KILIMANJARO

KILIMANJARO

The Great White Mountain of Africa

David Pluth • Mohamed Amin • Graham Mercer

Camerapix Publishers International

First published in 2001 by
Camerapix Publishers International
P.O. Box 45048
Nairobi, Kenya

ISBN: 1-874041-64-4

This book was designed and produced by
Camerapix Publishers International
P.O. Box 45048
Nairobi, Kenya

Production Manager: Rukhsana Haq

Edited by: Jan Hemsing, Roger Barnard,
Kantai Parseleo, Ian Vincent

Design Consultant: Craig Dodd

Design: Sam Kimani, Rachel Musyoni

Production Assistant: Joseph Kisilu

Colour Separations: Universal Graphics Pte Ltd, Singapore
Printed By: Atlas Printing Press
               Dubai, United Arab Emirates

Half-title: Climbers descending from the summit.
Title-page: A view of Kibo and the Great Baramco.
Contents: Approaching the summit ridge with the
snow-covered crater in the background.

Dedication

For 'Mo', without whom this book would not have been written, and to whom
Kilimanjaro was much more than a mountain.
And for Brian, who as an editor was so kind and encouraging.

Acknowledgements

While preparing the text for this book I was assisted by a number of people who helped with
their time and with their knowledge and experiences of Africa's Great White Mountain. These
include Tanzania's Minister for Natural Resources and Tourism, the Rt. Honourable Mrs. Zakia
Meghji M.P; Chief Park Wardens and rangers of Kilimanjaro National Park over the past two
decades and all the porters and guides operating on Kilimanjaro; Mr. Thomas Marealle; the late
Ms. Erica von Lany; Mrs. Peggy Bryce-Bennett; Seamus and Jackie Bryce-Bennett; all management
and staff of the Marangu, Kibo and Capricorn Hotels, Marangu, and the Y.M.C.A. Moshi; Dr. Alan
Rodgers (who was kind enough to proof-read this book and cruel enough to be honest); Mr.
Ernest Polack (a true gentleman whose love for, and acquaintance with, the mountain was an
inspiration); Ms. Jamila Sumra; Ms. Areta Williams; Patricia Mawalla; the late and eternally cheerful
Aloys Massawe; Raksha and Navnit Shah; Kabir and Hasina Hyderali; Julius Mlay of the Kilimanjaro
N.P. bookshop; and all those people, including Barry Whittemore, Kevin Bartlett, John Boyce, Bill
and Colin Powell, Claudia Hochstrasse, Kathy Dawson, Ms. Martha Hans, and my wife Anjum, who
have enjoyed or endured Kilimanjaro, at close hand or at a respectable distance, in my company.
Graham Mercer

––––––––––––––––––

A photographer's job on a book and a mountain of this magnitude is never easy and I would like
to sincerely thank the people from all walks of life who I met during the course of my work, from
the friendly taxi-drivers of Arusha and Moshi to the courteous staff at the entrance gates to
Kilimanjaro National Park. Throughout, Tanzania National Parks generously offered me assistance
and, in particular, I would like to thank Gerald Bigurube (at the time Acting Director General) and
James Lembeli (Head of Public Relations) for their continuing support, co-operation and faith in
the project. Thanks also to the late Mohamed Amin, one of the world's great photojournalists,
for encouraging me in my work; to Rukhsana Haq of Camerapix who has diligently pursued this
project; to Michael Chessler for offering warm words of encouragement; to Ian Vincent for setting
the tone for the style from the start; to Geert Lemmen of Sabena and Juma Yusuf of Air Tanzania
for help with transporting my equipment and to Sotar Mushi of Sopa Lodges for its importation;
to Buck Tilley for the keys to his house; to Willy Chambulo for arranging my trips on the mountain
and to my guide, Sancho (Steven Moita), and his family of assistants and porters who cheerfully
soaked, froze and exhausted themselves daily so we could get our pictures. Thanks go, as well,
to Andreas Naef and team at Studio 13 for developing my film; to Dennis Yee and Ivo Crivelli at
Foto Ganz for their ideas and obscure bits of hardware; to Paul Merki at Light & Byte for his
indestructible Lightware camera bags; and to Canon and Hasselblad, the makers of my cameras.
Finally, once again and always, I have to thank my wife Patricia for her sweet patience and
endless understanding that the life of a photographer has lots of ups, downs and absences, but
she knows she's always in my heart.
David Pluth

CONTENTS

Above: *The snow covered mountain from Maasailand on the Kenyan side of the border.*

Foreword

I first climbed Kilimanjaro some 35 years ago, at the tender age of fifteen, and whilst I have known many of the latter day personalities mentioned in the text, it is still fascinating to glean different snippets of information about them, for at last a detailed history / information / guide / picture book has been written as a single volume. The book opens with the birth of the mountain, and covers all aspects of its geological history up to the present day. The recent history and the beliefs and traditions of the native peoples living around the mountain's lower slopes are covered in detail, along with the stories of the various explorers from the 19th century who attempted to ascend this mountain, finally succeeding in 1889. Early 20th century climbers and pioneers are likewise covered and the concluding section is a detailed description on the present day tourist routes up to the summit.

Today, climbers attempting the ascent of Kilimanjaro face a very different mountain to what those intrepid explorers faced. Equipment quality these days is far superior to what was available to Meyer and Purtscheller when they climbed, more so is the fact that the mountain itself is a far cry from what it was in those days, for even in the time since I first climbed the mountain, huge changes to the climatic and hence glaciological conditions have taken place, and continue to do so. The ice is in rapid retreat, and one no longer has obstacles such as ice barriers to climb over or around on any of the three walking ascents. Indeed, one can regularly walk to the summit point without even touching snow, let alone glacial ice.

One hope I do have with this book is that, perhaps, somebody in the Tanzanian National Parks Authority - the minister herself maybe?, might read, or even browse through it, admire the photographs, and again, perhaps by some miracle, come to realise what a marvellous and wonderful "Asset" the people of Tanzania have. The visitors will then start to see some better care being taken in preserving what is a very fragile and delicate environment. To address just the litter, garbage and accommodation problem would be a start. It's not that the money is not available, after all a visitors pay hundreds of dollars just to enter the park. The problem is the money doesn't get invested back into the park. It is however "Africa" so perhaps one hopes in vain!!

Altogether, though, this is a comprehensive account, and for me, as I'm sure it will be for others knowledgeable about the area, it is heartening to see that there are still many pristine and unspoilt areas still to be found. I congratulate the authors on a splendid work which has long been needed.

Mark Savage

Introduction

Kilimanjaro, highest mountain in all Africa, dominates the north-eastern marches of Tanzania and the adjacent plains of south-eastern Kenya. If you were to stand at its snow-encrusted summit, with an unrestricted view in all directions, you would gaze down upon a remarkable tract of land, its limits defined only by the curvature of the earth and the haze of distance, a distance determined in part by the height of your vantage point, 19,336 feet (5,895 metres) above the plains; and on the same grand scale, for the snows of Kilimanjaro, given the right conditions, are visible from a distance of two hundred kilometres.

At the edge of your personal universe, away to the west and probably indiscernible in the dust-clouded horizons above the Great Rift, rise the eastern slopes of Ngorongoro; to the north, the universe ends where Nairobi begins; to the east, the eye commands a world which stretches two thirds of the way to Mombasa and the coast; and to the south, the observer is king as far as the Kitwei Plains, at the heart of the Maasai Steppe.

The people after which the Steppe was named encircle the mountain, and also their erstwhile enemies, the Chagga, who live on its lower slopes. Both peoples would still, in many ways, be recognizable to the nineteenth century explorers, though the Chagga, the true inheritors of Kilimanjaro, no longer dress in skins or carry spears and shields, nor do many of them now live in traditional beehive huts. The Maasai have also changed, but not so much. At least, not those who still pasture their precious cattle out on the plains below Kilimanjaro. Yet the Chagga can still strike a hard bargain, as in the old days, and the Maasai, constrained as they are by laws and bureaucracy and cultural decline, can still strike fear into the hearts of those who cross them, be they men or marauding lions.

Neither of these people know the mountain which commands their homelands as Kilimanjaro. The Chagga, who are mostly clustered on its southerly slopes, have no name for the whole massif, only for its two peaks, the highest of which, and shaped like a Christmas pudding they call *Kipoo* (rhyming with 'flow', not 'flew') and *Kimawensi*, lower by two thousand feet and much more rugged. In English and Swahili the peaks are known as Kibo and Mawenzi respectively. The Maasai know it as *Oldoiny'oibor*, the White Mountain, or as Ngaje Ngai, the House of God. Kilimanjaro is a Swahili word, a name bestowed, no doubt, by the Arab and Swahili caravan masters, one of whose trails (or 'lines') passed through the lands of the Chagga, on the way from the coast to the interior.

Its name, as we shall see, is worth closer scrutiny, but whatever its implications, the mountain itself remains Africa's highest, and perhaps its most beautiful. Seen from Moshi, with a full moon silvering its legendary snows; or from Kilaguni in Kenya's Tsavo West, where it forms the southernmost cusp of a remarkable volcanic panorama; or across Arusha National Park's Momella Lakes at dawn, the low sun lighting Kibo's eastern glaciers and transfusing its western flanks with a gradated rosy glow; or from the road which skirts Tanzania's north Pare Mountains, from where a driver might see, as the clouds lift, the White Mountain suddenly shouldering upwards from a grey-green sea of hills. Like Melville's Great White Whale, Kilimanjaro is supreme. There is no mountain on earth quite like it.

Considering its height and bulk and prepossessing beauty, considering that its snows are visible from as far away as two hundred kilometres, and must have been familiar to generations of caravaneers from the coast, it is all the more astonishing that the existence of Kilimanjaro was not officially revealed to the west until 1848. And that even then its 'discoverer', Johannes Rebmann, was scorned by some of the most distinguished geographers of the age.

Opposite: Engraving of Hans Meyer's triumphant 'conquering' of the summit on his first ascent; from his book.

Rebmann was a missionary, not a mountaineer, and never ventured higher than Kilimanjaro's foothills. But thirteen years after his momentous revelation a fellow German, Baron Karl Klaus von der Decken, confirmed the phenomenon of snows only three degrees south of the equator. Soon afterwards another missionary, Charles New, became the first known person to leave his footprints in the snows themselves. A succession of explorers, missionaries, adventurers and climbers followed, leaving their own ephemeral impressions higher and higher in the snows, until at last, in October 1889, Hans Meyer and Ludwig Purtscheller became the first known conquerors of the great White Mountain.

They, in turn, were followed by other climbers, including some of the world's most outstanding mountaineers, members of that perverse band of brothers (and latterly sisters) who are not content with reaching summits, but who have to make things difficult, and sometimes dangerous for themselves, by pioneering different and often demanding routes. But above all Kilimanjaro, or at least Kibo, is a mountain of the people, one of the few high peaks which seems to have been made for the man – and woman – in the street. As many as 10,800 visitors set foot on the mountain each year, only a small percentage of whom are serious climbers. This is not to say that every person who attempts Kilimanjaro is unaccomplished, but that in mountaineering terms, most of those who emulate Meyer's first triumph do so with little more technical equipment than a walking stick, and little more knowledge of mountaineering than the use of the stick demands.

But all of them, whatever else they have achieved or not achieved in life, have one thing in common with both the connoisseurs, and with everyone else, past or present, who has lived in or passed through this corner of Tanzania; they have all set foot, or at least eyes, on a most exceptional mountain in one of the world's most extraordinary countries. And they have witnessed, at first hand or from a distance, the 'miracle' of a mountain rising from the tropic plains and being capped with ice – the captivating snows of Kilimanjaro.

Left: Kibo at dawn after a night of heavy snowfall; from Rongai, on the Tanzania/ Kenya border.

Born In Hell, Raised in Eden

The origins and geographical
context of Kilimanjaro

Kilimanjaro's geological background

Great mountains, like great men, are often born of tumultuous times. Kilimanjaro is such a mountain. And, despite its apparent tranquillity the violence of its birth goes on. Terrible forces are at work, tearing Africa asunder. From the Dead Sea to the Zambezi the land is on the rack, stretched beyond what it can bear as the great tectonic plates that support it slide inexorably apart. Africa is cracking up from stress, and the Great Rift Valley, visible from space, is the outward sign of breakdown on the stoical face of a long-suffering continent.

The forces that created Kilimanjaro would have been understood by the ancient astrologers, for they are truly elemental – Fire, Earth, Air and Water. Conceived from earth and fire, the mountain's more distant future was shaped also by air and water. Its incandescent entry into the world was predetermined – its present bulk bestrides an intersection of major fault lines which extend along the North Pare Mountains and the Lelatema Escarpment to the south, and to the west the ragged column of mighty volcanic mounds and cones which begins with Mount Meru and stretches through Monduli and across the Great Rift towards Esimingor and the Ngorongoro Crater highlands.

The Rift reached its present form between one and two million years ago, before the fault line to the east ripped open in an explosive fusion of fire, molten rock and sulphurous smoke. At the end of this cataclysmic fury Kilimanjaro arose, its triumvirate of cones welling out hot lava over thousands of years while its peaks reached estimated heights of about 5,000 metres. The Shira cone collapsed into quiescence while Kibo and Mawenzi continued to rise to about 5,500 metres, their lava flows combining, between the two erupting peaks to form the basis of the intervening ridge that we now know as the Saddle. Mawenzi, almost literally, burned itself out, leaving Kibo to pour out its heart in a further series of eruptions. The most extensive of these, some 360,000 years ago, flooded the old Shira caldera with a black lava, known as rhomb porphyry. This dark viscous lava fanned out over the Saddle, around the base of the eroded Mawenzi and far to the north and south.

Kibo grew to about 5,900 metres and then, 300,000 years or so after its explosive birth, died out. Sporadic eruptions still broke out but from that time onwards the shaping of Kilimanjaro was largely determined by air and water, the latter sometimes in the form of ice. The whole mountain began to shrink and continues to do so, though not, perhaps, at as fast a rate as some of its would-be conquerors would wish. The bare, eroded massif was colonised by plants, led by those hardy pioneers, the grasses, to be followed by scrub, woodland, forest and moorland. These were soon colonised by animal life.

Kilimanjaro is not as geologically isolated as its appearance suggests, nor did the volcanic activity which caused it come to an end with its creation. The Great Rift was formed over twenty million years or so, with major faulting taking place within the last 10,000 years. Kilimanjaro, though not obviously part of the Rift Valley system, is linked to it by subterranean lava flows. It is just one member (and not, in terms of age, a very senior one) of a huge family of volcanoes, many of them active or semi-active, which blister the face of East Africa along the 9,700 kilometres of the Rift disfigurement.

Northern Tanzania is studded with these orphans of violence, created when deep fractures in the earth's crust were quickly inundated with a particularly fluid form of magma which cools to a tough black lava known as 'flood basalt', a substance best appreciated today in the famous archaeological site at Olduvai Gorge where it forms the stream-bed.

Opposite: The firepit at the centre of the crater leads to the head of the volcano.

Previous pages: Mt. Mawenzi at dawn from across the saddle.

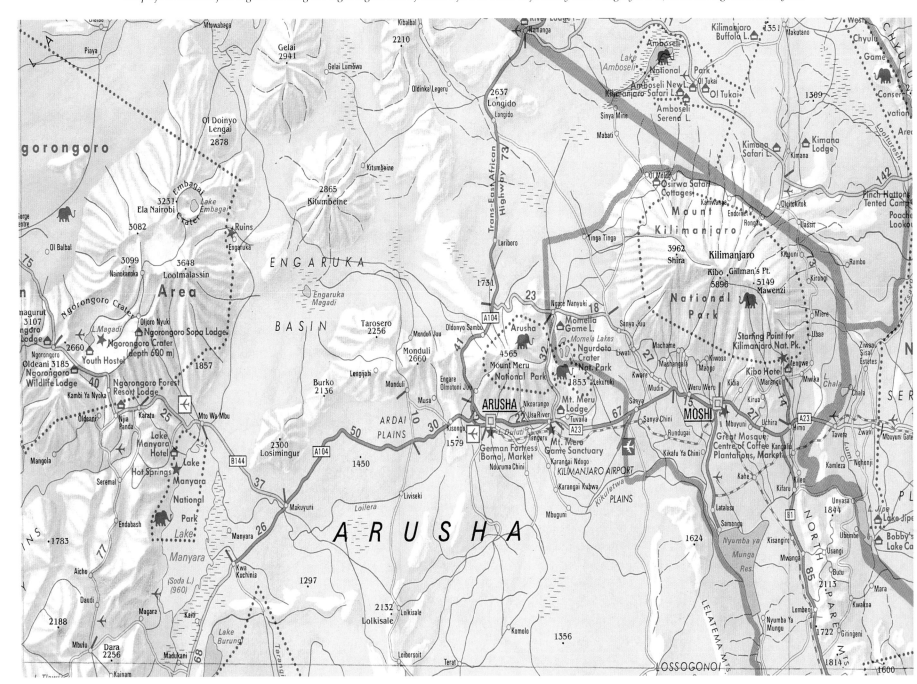

Amid the turbulence of the Rift's formation, enormous pressures and strains were built up and explosively released, spewing up large numbers of individual and composite volcanic cones. Many of them lie in what is now southern Maasailand, and have Maasai names. Names, appropriately for volcanoes, to fire the imagination – *Oldeani*, Mountain of Bamboo; *Sirua*, Mountain of the Eland; *Lolmolasin*, Mountain of the Gourds and *Kerimasi*, the Speckled Brow – all of which are to be found in the Crate Highlands around that most celebrated of all craters, Ngorongoro, the origin of whose name, like that of Kilimanjaro, remains a mystery.

Down in the Rift itself rise *Tarosero* and *Purko*, named after Maasai clans; *Esimingor*, the Wildcat; *Kitumbei*, the name of a plant which grows there; *Gelai*; and *Oldoinyo Lengai*, the Mountain of God, Tanzania's only active volcano. On the eastern wall of the Rift stands *Monduli*, and further east, behind the township of Arusha. *Oldoiny'orok*, the Black Mountain, or Mount Meru as it is commonly known. East again of Meru, behind another, smaller township, Moshi, towers the greatest of them all, *Oldoiny'oibor*, Africa's Great White Mountain, Kilimanjaro.

Above: Top of the Western Breach with a view west to Mt. Meru.

Kilimanjaro's wider geographical setting

On a clear day, as we have seen, an observer on Kibo's summit might look down upon a roughly circular landscape four hundred kilometres and more in diameter. Ignoring for the moment the mountain itself, the land he or she would overlook is part of a plateau which extends across most of the African interior at a mean altitude of about 1,500 metres above sea level. In this region it is an immense mosaic of grassland, open thornbush, riverine forest and cultivation traversed by a simplistic web of roads and tracks, and broken by a few rivers and the occasional lake. From its rolling expanses rise numerous hills and mountains, some of ancient crystalline rock, others more recent and volcanic, their shapely profiles pleasing to the eye and giving some perspective to the view.

From the plains these landscapes are amongst the most attractive in the world with their long, low-slung horizons and wide-angle skies. Away to the west lies the Great Rift, its forlorn beauty in places as striking as its geological significance. Closer at hand, above the town of Arusha, rises the dark, irregular pile of Mount Meru, its saw-toothed peak only 27 feet (9 metres) short of 15,000 feet (4,565 metres). Very different mountains, lengthy and angular, rise in a series of ridges which are slender and humped as gigantic chameleons just to the south-east of Kilimanjaro.

The valley which separates these ridges from Kilimanjaro, now peaceful and cultivated, was known, during the East African campaign of the first World War, as the Kilimanjaro Gap. Its southern ramparts are formed by the outriders of the North and South Pare mountains which give way, further south, to the Western Usambaras that are flanked, as one might guess, by the Eastern Usambaras. All are part of a long and discontinuous chain of similar block-fault mountains known collectively as the Eastern Arc. Each isolated range, as its forests have become cut off from those which once stretched across the breadth of Africa, has produced an astonishing number of endemic and near-endemic plants and animals that make these 'islands in the clouds' as unique, if not as well-known, as their oceanic equivalents such as the Galapagos archipelago.

Through the Kilimanjaro Gap on its Kenyan side lies the Kenyan border town of Taveta, for centuries a favourite resting place for slave and ivory traders who had recently crossed – or were about to recross – the waterless Taru Desert (which is part of the present-day Tsavo West National Park) on their way from Mombasa to the interior or vice versa. In the late 19th century, explorers such as Joseph Thomson delighted in the comforts of its forest glades and bubbling streams, not to mention those of its scantily clad young women among whom (according to Thomson) 'conjugal fidelity' was unknown. Missionary-explorers such as Johannes Rebmann, the first to have seen Kilimanjaro, presumably restricted themselves to more innocent pleasures, often after suffering privations that John the Baptist might have baulked at. Rebmann, for example, crossed the Taru eighteen times in as many months, once in his stockinged feet. The starkly glorious thornbush east of Taveta, from which Rebmann first sighted the snows of Kilimanjaro, is now, like the Taru, part of the Tsavo West National Park where, in its south-western corner and below the North Pare mountains, gleams Lake Jipe, from the shores of which Kilimanjaro looks particularly high and handsome.

Another Kenyan wildlife sanctuary which almost claims Kilimanjaro as its own is Amboseli National Park, located at the north-west foot of the mountain. Formerly administered by the local Maasai council and now managed by the Kenya Wildlife Service, Amboseli is a large tract of open thornbush, swamp and plain where the finest of dry season dust blows every which way on the slightest of breezes. It is part of a great triangle composed mostly of open grasslands still roamed by the Maasai and their herds in the westerly sector, and becoming increasingly fenced into ranches and farms to the east.

Opposite: Climbers returning to camp after exploring their surroundings.

Above: *Mt. Meru rises from the plains at sunset.*

Above: Mawenzi's jagged peak, foreground, with the ice-capped dome of Kibo behind it.

Opposite: Cl[...] ringing Shira [...]

The triangle has the Arusha-Voi road as its base and Nairobi at its apex.

South of Kilimanjaro, to complete the circle, the Maasai Steppe rolls away to central Tanzania. It is bounded in the east and south by the Pangani River which flows below the splendid outlines of the Pare and Usambara mountains before making a dash for the Indian Ocean south of Tanga. Its western borders coincide, more or less, with the Dodoma-Arusha highway, part of the Tanzanian section of the Great North Road. From this road, as it curves towards Arusha, the lucky, late afternoon traveller can watch the soft light of the setting sun brush pastel colours over the western aspects of Africa's highest mountain. Which is where we – and Kilimanjaro – come in.

In the days of the explorers, many of whom passed through the incomparable lands that still encircle Kilimanjaro, the bush and grassland and forest abounded with game. Rhino were especially common. Even now, though the rhino has more or less disappeared due to its poaching for the supposed benefits of its fibrous horn, much wildlife remains. Large elephant herds can still be encountered in the Tsavo wildernesses, and in Tarangire National Park in the north-west corner of the Maasai Steppe. And elephant and buffalo still roam the slopes of Kilimanjaro and Meru, and feed on the sedges of the Amboseli swamps. Leopard are to be found everywhere, in and outside the sanctuaries, and so are lion, these big cats preying on the buffalo, zebra and great variety of antelopes which have survived human incursions, sometimes inconsiderable numbers. The giraffe still delights the eye, here and there, its unlikely height paradoxically emphasised, rather than scaled down, by the stupendous backdrop of the great White Mountain which, of all the features and wonders of this well-countenanced land, is the undisputed overlord.

Footsteps in the Snows of Time

A brief history of the exploration, political events and climbing expeditions on and around Kilimanjaro

The exploration of Kilimanjaro in the second half of the 19th century.

A human skull estimated to be one million years old was found in the mid-1990s in Eritrea. It is said to have features characteristic of *Homo sapiens,* and though the scientists involved warn that their assessments are preliminary, they seem convinced that their discovery supports the theory that traits of modern man had begun to differentiate in Africa 300,000 years earlier than had been previously thought. It also seems to support the theory that modern man evolved in East Africa, spreading into the wider world about 100,000 years ago. As northern Tanzania is one of the richest sources of evidence of early man, it is quite feasible, even probable, that Kilimanjaro's explosive entry into the world was witnessed by our human ancestors. For the mountain is a mere 750,000 years old, give or take a few millennia. Its formative eruptions must have been quite a sight. Yet this eminently visible equatorial giant, known to some form of man for the greater part of one million years, remained unknown to the 'sophisticated' western world until the middle of the 19th century.

It was not that East Africa itself was remote or rarely visited. From before the time of Christ a succession of traders from as far away as China, Arabia and Europe had regular contact with the towns and settlements along the East African coast, known in those far-off days as the Land of Zinj. Kilimanjaro was a focal point of at least one of the caravan routes which supplied these coastal communities. Swahili and Arab caravan leaders returning from the interior had spoken often of a mountain with a 'silver' summit. But the only references to its existence – and those were vague – were made by the Alexandrian geographer and astronomer Ptolemy, around 100 AD, who wrote of 'a great snow mountain' lying inland from Rhapta (probably present-day Pangani); by the 13th century Arab geographer, Abu'l Fida who also mentioned a mountain that was white in colour; by a Chinese writer in about 1400 AD, who noted that the country to the west of Zanzibar 'reaches to a great mountain'; and by the Portuguese geographer Fernandes de Encisco who in 1519 also reported that 'the Ethiopian Mount Olympus, which is very high' rose somewhere to the west of Mombasa.

In 1846 the man who was to confirm these speculations, Johannes Rebmann, a 26-year-old missionary from Württemberg, joined his German compatriot and fellow-missionary, Johann Ludwig Krapf, at the mission station of Rabai Mpya outside Mombasa. Both men burned with a spiritual obsessiveness that would be brutally exposed to the indifference of Africa. Krapf's young wife and new-born daughter died of malaria soon after their arrival, with Krapf lying helpless with the same fever in the same room, and Rebmann was blind by the time he left Africa in 1873. Far worse, from the evangelical point of view, was the fact that converts to Christianity were to be almost as rare as snowflakes on this sweltering Islamic coast.

Yet they were remarkable men who achieved much. They would take it in turns to explore the interior, attempting to spread the gospel. They travelled in stark contrast to later expeditions by the more famous explorers – Stanley, prior to his last expedition, had telegraphed his Zanzibar agent to hire 600 porters and purchase vast amounts of goods for barter, including 27,000 yards of cloth, a ton-and-a-half of beads and a ton of brass, copper and steel wire. The cloth and wire were to be given to various chiefs and headmen as 'hongo' – the 19th century African equivalent of airport tax on an even more extortionate scale – as the caravans passed through tribal lands. Krapf and Rebmann were destitute by comparison. Rebmann, tough enough to tackle the Taru desert in stockinged feet, was reduced to tears by the demands for 'hongo' by the Chagga chief Mamkinga. At the outset of another expedition into the same country his guide had stared

Opposite: Maasai warrior in fighting gear, an old print made about the time of the first ascent of Kilimanjaro.

Previous pages: Climbing to the top of the Western Breach.

with incredulity at the missionary's nine porters, informing Rebmann that caravans never went to Chaggaland with less than a hundred armed men. 'But you', he had said, 'are here with nothing but an umbrella'. And, he might have added, a lot of courage and faith.

There were, for the missionaries, a few rainbows against the gloom. One Sunday in May, 1848, with his nine men and the umbrella, Rebmann found himself in what is still, especially after the rains, one of the most wildly beautiful parts of Africa, close to the Ngulia and Taita hills, an area now partially absorbed into Kenya's Tsavo West National Park. 'It seemed to me', Rebmann recorded, 'as if Nature were celebrating with me the Sabbath. Mountains and all hills; fruitful trees; beasts and all cattle; creeping things, and flying fowl with the varied melody of their song, praised the Creator with me'.

Four days later, at about 10 o'clock on the morning of 11 May, Rebmann witnessed a sight even more uplifting. Sixty or seventy miles to the west, the 'mountains of Jagga' were clearing, and the young missionary 'fancied I saw the summit of one of them covered with a dazzlingly white cloud. My guide called the white which I saw, merely *'Beridi'*, cold; it was perfectly clear to me, however, that it could be nothing else but snow'. His laconic guide, the remarkable but unsung Swahili caravan leader Bwana Kheri, could not have known that snow, three degrees south of the equator, was something to write home about. And what was 'perfectly clear' to poor Rebmann was not going to be perfectly clear to some of Europe's eminent geographers, especially the Englishman William Desborough Cooley.

The question of snow at the equator was not in itself the issue; geographers were well aware of the snow-clad peaks in the Andes. What was in doubt was the height of mountains in East Africa. Self-appointed experts such as Cooley, who from his leather-upholstered armchair in the lounge of the Royal Geographical Society (or somewhere similar) derided Rebmann's claims as 'betraying weak powers of observation, strong fancy, an eager craving of wonders, and childish reasoning. Those eternal snows, he went on, '. . . have so little of shape and substance, and appear so severed from realities, that they take on quite a spectral character'.

The snows of Kilimanjaro were rather more substantial to another German, Baron Karl Claus von der Decken, who not only saw them thirteen years after Rebmann but who, the following year, actually climbed to about 14,000 feet on the mountain where he encountered a somewhat less than spectral snowstorm. He and his companion, Dr. Otto Kersten were, incidentally, the first non-Africans to climb beyond the forest zone. Cooley remained unimpressed – after all Rebmann and von der Decken were not just foreign but German in an age when God Himself was not only English but a member of the Tory party. Cooley dismissed the Baron as an 'eccentric traveller'. This was not wholly inaccurate as the wealthy young Baron liked his comforts and, long before embarking for the summit, had polished off the magnum of champagne which had been intended for the moment of triumph. Which might – or might not – explain why he didn't make it.

'So opportune a fall of snow!', Cooley had crowed, but Sir Roderick Murchison, president of the Royal Geographical Society who had previously shared, with many others, Cooley's intransigent opinions, at last acknowledged that Rebmann had been right all along. The missionary was vindicated. Cooley (one hopes) was humbled and von der Decken was awarded the Society's coveted gold medal.

The controversies over Kilimanjaro and its snows were closely connected with the question of the Nile. The age-old mystery of its source, control of which would give control over Egypt with all its political and strategic advantages, had aroused emotions and interest on a scale, and of an intensity, difficult now to comprehend. For centuries geographers had theorised and argued about the origins of the sacred river. The obsession was reaching fever pitch when Rebmann had, inadvertently, given it a new and not altogether welcome focus; the existence of a huge, snow-topped mountain, only one hundred and seventy miles from the coast, began to threaten a few cherished theories. Was it not possible that the melt-waters and streams of such a mountain might feed into the Nile? But in the same year that Baron von der Decken had confirmed Rebmann's discovery mystery John Hanning Speke had announced, after seeing the outflow of Lake Victoria from his vantage point overlooking Ripon Falls, that 'The question of Nile is settled'.

It was far from settled, as it happened. Speke's claim was met with the same incredulity, from some quarters, as Rebmann's had been. But enough people supported Speke for the ardour to fade from the age-old arguments. Kilimanjaro, for the time being, also faded into the clouds of history, though in August 1871 another missionary, this time an English Methodist named Charles New, had toiled up the mountain. He had not, we may assume, seen off a magnum of champagne en route, and had gone one better than the more bibulous baron to reach the snow line, then at about 14,500 feet (4,420 metres).

He hadn't stayed around to celebrate. His guides had fallen by the wayside, one by one, as the air grew thinner and colder. The last man to drop out had excused himself with a line worth remembering, especially by those of us who struggle up Kilimanjaro and long to turn back without losing face. '. . . the ascent of this mountain', he had said, with great self-sacrifice, 'is nothing to me, but I do not want you to be beaten'.

Other Chaggas had questioned the missionary's sanity before he had even set off. 'Who are you', they had asked, 'that you should ascend the mighty Kilima Njaro?' And he himself, as he plodded upwards alone, had been overcome by oppressive sensations '. . . at the idea of profound solitude, of standing on heights to which no human being had ever before ascended . . .' Then, having become the first known person to plant his footsteps in the high snows, he had chopped away a few chunks to give to his men before hurrying down to rejoin them. The Chagga (they are known for their enterprise) had wanted to sell them as medicine, and had been astonished when the white man said that the substance would soon disappear in the heat. '. . . they smiled incredulously', New tells us, saying 'Who ever heard of stones melting?'

In the early 1880s Kilimanjaro again began to attract the attention of European adventurers and naturalist/explorers. Significantly, with the scramble for Africa looming on the political horizon, the more notable contestants were German and British. Dr Gustav Fischer passed through the area in 1882 on his way to 'discover' Lake Naivasha. He was followed, in 1883, by the young Scot, Joseph Thomson. Charles Miller, in his highly readable 'Lunatic Express' is tempted to ask whether Thomson 'should have been allowed to go off by himself without a keeper'. Certainly the Scotsman had more than a touch of whimsy in his character. But he possessed a scholarly mind and the instincts of an outstanding leader.

Having enjoyed a fortnight resting and admiring the girls in what he described as the 'little African Arcadia of Taveta', Thomson travelled to Moshi and from there 'set off at a killing pace' to get as far as he could up Kilimanjaro in a single day. And to collect what plants he could at the higher altitudes. 'After seven hours of climbing, the most severe I have ever experienced', Thomson was still below 9000 feet and still in the rainforest. Reluctantly he turned back, 'to rush down

Above: The slopes of Kibo rising from the saddle.

the mountain at a headlong pace, picking up at intervals my broken-down followers'. He went on to make a name for himself as the first outsider to cross Maasailand.

The next European to make a name for himself in the shadow of Kilimanjaro was equally young – only twenty-six when he had first set foot on the mountain. He was small, erudite and energetic, and rather less distracted than Thomson. His name, Harry Johnston might have suggested to his class-conscious English compatriots a builder's labourer from the provinces. His full name was Henry Hamilton Johnston, which would have reassured them. He was 'officer material'. He would eventually be knighted in recognition of his outstanding services as a colonial administrator and was already, at twenty-six, a most unusual man. He had explored Tunisia before his twenty-first birthday, Angola at twenty-five and was still in his twenty-sixth year when he had bumped into Stanley in the Congo.

Johnston quickly established himself on Kilimanjaro. But first he needed to win the patronage of one of the most eminent of Chagga chieftains, Mandara, known to the Chagga as Rindi. Rindi, notoriously fickle and greedy to those explorers and travellers who upset him but beloved and respected by his supporters, had given Charles New a particularly hard time. There was to be friction, too, between the chief and Johnston but, to begin with, everything in the garden was coming up roses. Or more accurately, turnips. Johnston had persuaded Rindi to let him have a small plot of land and 'within weeks had constructed a three-roomed cottage for himself, quarters for his men and a poultry yard; he had sown a kitchen garden with tomatoes, onions, turnips, potatoes, cucumbers and melons'. In his spare time he had achieved what he had come to do – rambled around the mountain collecting specimens of plants and animals, making notes and exercising his considerable artistic talents.

Johnston was later tempted, by the upstart Chief of Marangu, Marealle, to leave Taveta for Marangu. Rindi was not best pleased, and Johnston himself, as he entered into Marealle's presence, must have had second thoughts about the move. He was obliged to present his credentials after crawling backwards to the audience chamber through a dark and narrow tunnel, emerging bottom-first before the chieftain and his attendants.

It is difficult to imagine the next man to attempt Kilimanjaro crawling in such a demeaning manner from a dank tunnel. Samuel Teleki von Szek was a Hungarian count of the Holy Roman Empire, a bon vivant and gourmet who specialised in the esoteric pastime of breeding 'tough horses with gazelle-like eyes and Arab heads'. He had been persuaded, by no less a personage than Crown Prince Rudolph, son of His Imperial and Apostolic Majesty Franz-Joseph I, Emperor of Austria, King of Hungary and a mouthful of other titles, to explore the lands north of Lake Baringo which Joseph Thomson had mentioned in his published book *Through Masai Land*. Prince Rudolph had also introduced Teleki to Ludwig von Höhnel, a Czech naval officer who was to become his travelling companion and lifelong friend.

On his way the count and his companion decided to 'take in' Kilimanjaro. By 19 June 1887 they were camping alone on the Saddle, the swayback ridge between Kilimanjaro's twin peaks, Kibo and Mawenzi. As the weather worsened and the evening temperature dropped towards minus eleven degrees Centigrade, Teleki and von Höhnel had somehow managed to dispose of a preserved ham and some ship's biscuits, washed down with mugs of cocoa and a bottle of red wine, before retiring for the night. Despite their thick woollen underclothes, heavy overcoats and warm blankets they scarcely slept through the bitter cold. Well before daybreak they decided that if they were going to be miserable they might as well be miserable on the move and, after warming themselves by a roaring fire and melting the frozen water in their flasks to make another mug of cocoa each, they set off for the summit.

At 16,240 feet von Höhnel had enough. 'Fully satisfied with all I had achieved,' he wrote, 'I yielded to my irresistible desire for sleep. . . I was awoken from a short deep slumber by a strong wind and the dazzling rays of the midday sun'. His companion had climbed on for a further hour until, at 17,387 feet, less than 2000 feet from the summit, he also had become temptingly sleepy, as many climbers do, and had turned for home. His inner ears were hurting, there was a rushing noise in his head and his lips were bleeding. He was soon back with von Höhnel and, after a quick stop at the tent for (of all things) another swig of wine and some more ship's biscuits, they had continued down the mountain. If they had suffered minor privations their porters, who had been sent back on their last legs from the Saddle, hadn't had much fun either – they had climbed to what is sometimes referred to as an Afro-Arctic desert 'In the garb of Adam' and with nothing but a bottle of milk to sustain them.

Conquest of Kilimanjaro – the first successful ascents of Kibo

The powerful British presence in Zanzibar and the later establishment of German East Africa gave impetus and support to the explorations and tentative ascents of Kilimanjaro that took place in the latter half of the 19th century. It is no surprise, then, that the highest mountain in Africa was first conquered by a German at a time when German rule was steeply in the ascendant. Two years earlier, Teleki and von Höhnel, nearing the Saddle during their own unavailing attempt, had paused by a stream at a little over 13,000 feet, the same stream which tourists now cross as they too head for Kibo after leaving Horombo Hut, and by which stands a sign announcing 'Last Water'. In June 1887 Teleki and von Höhnel had found 'The water murmuring underneath a springy bed of turf several inches thick, and so close and firm that we could stand upon it. . . . There was a good deal of ice about this spring too, although the temperature of the water was +7 degrees Centigrade'.

A few weeks later, in July, a German geographer, Dr Hans Ludwig Meyer, had named the Stream *Schneequelle*, 'Snow stream', as it bubbled from a drift of snow. There were drifts six feet deep on the southern slopes of the Saddle – Teleki and von Höhnel (not to mention their stark-naked porters) had been lucky to have missed them. Meyer and his companion Eberstein had encountered mists, sleet and extensive fields of ice a little further up the mountain. Eberstein, like von Höhnel the previous month, had succumbed to exhaustion after a gallant struggle through the poor conditions. Meyer had gone on, reaching about 18,000 feet (5,500 metres) and within one-and-a-half thousand feet of the summit. He had there been confronted by a steep slope of fragmented ice leading to a solid ice-wall, blue among the swirls of sleet and grey-white mist, and towering almost a hundred feet above him. For the best of modern mountaineers it might have posed no lasting problem; for Meyer, alone and with limited equipment, it had been too much.

But Meyer was a most determined man. In September 1889 he had returned, accompanied by an experienced and respected Alpine guide, Ludwig Purtscheller, and a mass of technical and mountaineering equipment. The equipment did not include Meyer's crampons, which had somehow wound up in Ceylon (later Sri Lanka) much to the bewilderment, one would imagine, of the Ceylonese customs officers. Relays of porters had scurried up and down to the party's base camp on the Kilimanjaro moorland, carrying, every three days, fresh provisions from Marangu, the small settlement on the lower slopes.

At half past two on the morning of 3 October Meyer and Purtscheller left their advance camp at 4,300 metres, in favourable conditions. They reached the snowline at about 5,000 metres an hour after sunrise. By 9 am they were up against the ice sheet which then covered the peak, and were obliged to ascend a steeply canted slope, hacking out steps in the solid ice. At that altitude the least exertion demands an effort of will, and every step required about twenty strokes of the axe. It took two hours to reach the smooth glacial ice beyond the shelf, but the two men were then faced with savagely sculptured icefields and crevasses choked with snow, into which they sometimes sank up to their armpits. The final stretch to the crater rim, a distance that on dry and level ground would have taken little more than a minute, took nearly two hours. Their feelings, as they stood on the edge of the crater which no human being had ever seen, must have been mixed. For despite their triumph the actual summit of Kilimanjaro, another one hundred metres higher, lay at least another hour-and-a-half away.

Weakened and wearied they staggered back to base camp. Not surprisingly they had a lie-in the next morning, snug

Opposite: The memorial to Hans Meyer at the park headquarters at Marangu.

in their sheepskin sleeping bags. The next day they moved the advance camp up to 4,600 metres and on the following morning, at 3 o'clock they set off again for the summit. With their route clearly marked and the steps in the ice-shelf already cut they made good progress and reached the crater rim just before 9 am. Soon they were standing at the highest point in Africa. Meyer planted a small German flag, the two men shook hands, raised three cheers for their Kaiser, and bestowed his name on the peak. Kaiser Wilhelm Spitze, 19,336 feet (5,895 metres) is now Uhuru Point, and is regularly conquered, sometimes by people who wouldn't recognise an ice-axe if they saw one.

Not that an ice-axe is needed on Kibo, at least on the popular walking routes. Mawenzi is a different matter, and it was to Mawenzi that Meyer and Purtscheller had turned a few days after mastering Kibo. They made three unsuccessful attempts on the summit, though the climbs represented valuable contributions to future ascents. Still not satisfied, Meyer and Purtscheller strode back across the Saddle and scaled the northern slopes of Kibo. At about 5,700 metres they came up against a very difficult wall of ice and retreated. Two days later, however, they tried another route to the east.

By 7.30 am they had reached the edge of the ice cap, where they discovered a convenient depression (now known as Hans Meyer Notch) in the thick mass of ice. Not long afterwards they were on the floor of Kibo's crater which was filled with ice and snow. Meyer described the scene as 'a spectacle of imposing majesty and unapproachable grandeur'. It must indeed have been a beautiful sight with slabs of ice stepping up towards the inner cone in glistening terraces of blue and white, they and the snows all shining in the morning sun, and a further field of ice, sliding, quite literally if imperceptibly, towards a breach in the western wall and into the glaciers beyond.

It was glaciers (and an enduring love for the mountain which meant so much to him) which took Meyer back to Kilimanjaro in 1898 to make a thorough study of the moving ice. He and his fellow-climber, Platz, reached the crater rim, the first ascent since Meyer's initial triumph. He found that the glaciers had retreated to extents of about a hundred metres. The ice in the crater had virtually disappeared, and with it much of the splendour of the scene he had witnessed only a decade before. Water was actually flowing into the crater from a melting glacier between the central cone and the northern wall. The ice was being sculpted into a new and angular beauty by the very process of melting, into a fantasia of turrets and towers, crevasses, caves and crenellations. Meyer stood astonished and predicted that within two or three decades Kibo would be clear of ice. He was wrong, though a hundred years later the ice was still withdrawing.

Whatever effects political changes have had upon the region, one thing at least has remained stable – the mountain itself. Despite Meyer's prophecy of 1898, Kibo's ice-cap survives though a century later it is noticeably diminished. What Meyer might also have underestimated, had he been asked, is the huge number of people who have followed in his footsteps. Between 1889, the year of Meyer's triumphal ascent, and 1927, only twenty-three people set foot on the peak. Many, as one might expect, were German. They included Captain Johannes Korner, who reached Gillman's Point by a route close to the present 'Marangu Route' (October 1898), and Lange and Weigle, who followed in Korner's footsteps but went on to make the second successful attempt on Kibo summit in July 1909. The climbs might have been few but they were important, with new routes being explored and opened up. The fourth ascent of Kibo was actually completed on skis by the Munich climber Fürtwangler and his fellow-skier König. Across the Saddle the peak of Mawenzi, named after Hans Meyer, was finally mastered by E Oehler and Fritz Klute, in July 1912. Interestingly enough, Mawenzi was

Above: An artist in Kibo Crater, from Hans Meyer's book.

first climbed by a woman, Sheila MacDonald, on July 28th 1927, a few days before she went on to become the first woman to climb Kibo. A German lady, Frau Von Ruckte-Schell, had reached Gillman's Point before the First World War.

By 1912 ascents of the lower slopes of Kilimanjaro were becoming easier, with the path from Marangu (now part of the 'Marangu' or 'Tourist Route') being established. Bismarck Hut (now Mandara) and Peters Hut (Horombo) had been built by Dr E. Forster for the German Kilimanjaro Mountain Club. Those huts are no longer in use but the sites, also part of the later 'Tourist Route', are still used as bases for walkers and climbers. The original Hans Meyer Cave, about ten minutes walk from the present Kibo Hut, was used as the final bivouac and was known as *Nyumba ya Mungu*, 'House of God', by the Chagga.

In 1926 the Reverend Dr R Reusch, a German missionary who had chosen to work in the Kilimanjaro area, became only the ninth known person since Meyer and Purtscheller to climb Kibo. He might have only just made the 'top ten' but what he lacked in priority he made up for by perseverance – he went on to climb Kilimanjaro about 50 times. He had another minor claim to fame (or notoriety) in the anecdotal annals of the mountain – it was Reusch who discovered the famous frozen leopard, mentioned in Hemingway's *Snows of Kilimanjaro* and remembered in the name 'Leopard Point', on the eastern rim of the crater, where the leopard was first discovered. Reusch became, perhaps, the first vandal of Kilimanjaro, cutting off one of the leopard's ears as a memento after attempting, unsuccessfully, to cut off the whole head. Later souvenir hunters apparently disposed of the rest of the animal.

In 1930 the famous Eric Shipton (known for planning Everest expeditions on used cigarette packets) took a wrong turning on Mawenzi with Bill Tilman, and made the first ascent of Nordecke Peak (5,140 metres/16,863 feet). They then descended and climbed Hans Meyer Peak. Just like that.

Colonial and post-independence influences in the Kilimanjaro region

Teleki and von Höhnel were among the few 19th-century explorers of Kilimanjaro who were neither German nor British. The predominance of these two super-powers reflected the growing interest, among western politicians and merchants, in East Africa and the sea lanes of the western Indian Ocean, particularly after the opening of the Suez Canal in 1869. Britain and Germany, almost by default, turned out to be the major protagonists. The various British or German-led missions, explorations and climbs, however much they might have been inspired by genuine philanthropy, geographical curiosity or personal challenge, were part of a larger political event which, in the 1880s, precipitated the 'Scramble for Africa'. Zanzibar, ruled directly by the Sultans of Oman since 1832, controlled much of the East African interior as well as the coast, and was growing increasingly prosperous from the ivory, slave and spice trade. Britain gradually won the trust and support of the Zanzibar Sultans, only to become the power behind the throne.

The Germans had their own imperial enthusiasts. Just a few months after Joseph Thomson had returned from his crossing of Maasailand in 1884, a less innocent man and his two German compatriots had arrived in Zanzibar with forged documents, and slipped away to the mainland. The leader of this trio, Carl Peters, was later described, with depressing accuracy, as being 'short on ethics and long on cruelty'. The three Germans were on the mainland for only a few weeks but by the time they left they had persuaded several African chiefs to sign away considerable chunks of their traditional lands. Britain's 'man in Zanzibar', John Kirk, was alarmed by this sudden challenge to British-backed authority in the region, but Peters' claims were backed by the German Chancellor, Bismarck, and the 'Scramble for Africa' had begun.

Germany's 'sphere of influence' in East Africa can be said to date officially from 1886, when the first Anglo-German agreement was signed. The colony (which until 1890 had no western boundaries) was to last only thirty years. In 1890 its borders, more or less coinciding with those of present-day Tanzania, were defined by a second Anglo-German treaty and by an 'arrangement' with Sultan Barghash of Zanzibar. Zanzibar was declared a British protectorate, but for four million German marks the Sultan surrendered his rights to that sector of the coastal strip which adjoined the German territories. German East Africa was a reality, with most of what is now Kenya ceded to the British. When the boundaries were drawn, it was decided that Kilimanjaro would be entirely within German territory – hence the blip in the otherwise ruler-straight border between Kenya and Tanzania. There seems to be no truth in the story that Queen Victoria handed over the mountain as a birthday present to Bismarck (her cousin), though it would have been a brave politician who opposed her had she made such wishes known.

Initially German East Africa was ruled, on behalf of 'The Iron Chancellor', with an iron hand, provoking resentment and retaliation among the natives. Kilimanjaro, and the Chagga chiefdoms who held sway on its lower slopes, saw a great deal of friction and fighting during the days of German rule, much of it described in the following chapter. In fairness it must also be said that the Germans did a great deal to develop their new colony, and their brief but intensive stay in the Kilimanjaro area left a legacy which wasn't, by any means, all negative. It was the Germans, in fact, who first officially protected Kilimanjaro, declaring it a game reserve early in the 20th century. And Chagga, always quick to absorb the more advantageous aspects of other cultures, soon appreciated Teutonic thoroughness, industry and initiative. The fact that the Kilimanjaro region remains one of the most advanced in Tanzania owes much to German influence and Chagga adaptability.

Opposite: Kilimanjaro rises above the farmland near Moshi.

The colonial powers taught the Chagga, and the East Africans in general, less constructive lessons. In 1914, Africans of British and German East Africa suddenly found themselves embroiled (on opposing sides) in the 'Great War' as it soon became known in Europe. The East African campaign, scornfully described as an 'Ice Cream War' by those British who saw it as a 'sideshow' that would soon 'melt away in the sun' was, in fact, as brutal and bitter in its own way as any conflict in the fields of Flanders; the differences were of degree rather than kind. The combatants were fighting for their lives, and the only ice-cream many of them saw was that on top of Kilimanjaro which witnessed, with its usual indifference, some of the initial encounters.

The valley known to the British Imperial forces as the Kilimanjaro Gap was of immense strategic importance, especially at the outset of the campaign. General Paul von Lettow-Vorbeck, the shrewd German commander, had controlled the area until the British and their allies, under Jan Smuts, forced the Gap early in 1916, pursuing (with only limited success) the German *schutztruppe* after being badly mauled during the taking of Salaita Hill, near Taveta. Salaita, and the later-cultivated valley which the opposing armies fought so desperately to control, are clearly visible from the slopes of Kilimanjaro. So is Lelatema, a range of hills just to the south of the mountain. It was wrested from German control, like Salaita, only after a ferocious battle; at one point a single officer and seventeen men of the Rhodesia Regiment clung to the newly-taken hills and held on until it was secured. Looking down upon the scene later in time, it is difficult to believe that these innocent fields and hills have such a bloody history.

Von Lettow's forces were never vanquished but, with their retreat south into Mozambique, their former colony was appropriated by the British who, by the close of 1916, had established a provisional administration. From 1920 they governed the country, then named Tanganyika, under a League of Nations mandate. It wasn't easy, as the erstwhile 'German East Africa' had suffered badly because of the war, the flu epidemic which followed and the world slump of the early 1920. But when Sir Donald Cameron took over as governor in 1925, Tanganyika was exporting twice as much as she had exported before the conflict, and was independent of British grants-in-aid.

Cameron was to be called 'the architect of modern Tanganyika'. His policy of government was directly opposite to that of the Germans, employing the well-tested British system of indirect rule which Cameron called 'native administration'. The system, delegating certain powers to paramount chiefs or headmen, caused problems with people such as the Chagga and the Maasai whose tribal structures were quite different, but on the whole Cameron comes across as an able, energetic and sincere administrator. He improved the road network and the economy and did much for education throughout Tanganyika, but his greatest single contribution to the Kilimanjaro region and the Chagga people, perhaps, was to encourage and develop the growing and marketing of coffee through locally owned cooperatives as well as individual expatriates.

British settlement in Tanganyika was never extensive, though Kilimanjaro was just as attractive to some British farmers as it had been to the Germans. But although independence came earlier than expected, on 9 December 1961, it was always anticipated, and Tanzania's first and best-known president, Julius Nyerere, inherited a country that was basically a poor and relatively undeveloped cousin of Kenya. In defence of the British, it must be remembered that Tanganyika was not, like Kenya, a colony, and that it was under British control for less than half a century. Even that

Above: Pointers to other parts of East Africa on the signboard in Arusha's clock tower round-about, the centre point between Cape Town and Cairo.

brief interlude was disrupted by the Great Depression of the late 1920s and early 1930s, and by the Second World War which broke out just as the economy was on the mend. That war had much less impact on Tanganyika in general, and the Kilimanjaro region in particular, than its predecessor, though it helped to raise the winds of change.

Kilimanjaro figured symbolically in the independence celebrations, when a Tanzanian was chosen to plant the national flag at the summit, renamed 'Uhuru Point', (Freedom Point) to commemorate the occasion. Kilimanjaro, however, decided to declare its own independence. Exceptionally foul weather and deep snowdrifts restricted the flag-raising ceremony to Gillman's Point, on the crater rim and 210 metres short of the summit. Twelve months later the flag was successfully relocated, but not before the initial failure had cast a symbolic shadow over Tanzania's own soon-to-be thwarted ambitions. The bright promise of the new nation was soon dimmed as Nyerere's 'African socialist' experiments – and with them Tanzania's economy – collapsed.

The Kilimanjaro region, thanks largely to the ingenuity and ebullient spirit of the Chagga, and to the natural fertility of their homeland, came through better than many other parts of the country. With the economic liberalisation which followed Nyerere's dignified decision to step down in 1985 the Chagga, natural 'free marketeers', began to focus their attention on new business opportunities within and beyond their mountain homelands. The Kilimanjaro region, like everywhere else in Tanzania, remains poor but its enterprising inhabitants, wherever they are based, are constantly poised to take advantage of any economic upsurge.

First ascent of Mawenzi and Kibo's Breach Wall

By 1937 the number of people reaching the top of Kibo had trebled, (Kibo Hut had been built in 1932) and the numbers multiplied so quickly that it became impossible to maintain accurate records. Among the more casual 'hill-walkers' were some genuine climbers, two of whom mastered Mawenzi seventy-five years after Meyer and Purtscheller's trio of failures on the same peak. The story of the conquest of Mawenzi involves an even more unusual animal 'find' than the leopard on Kibo. It also demanded some pretty stiff climbing.

The summit of Kibo can be reached by people who have no mountaineering experience, without so much as a walking stick to assist them. No one walks to the top of Mawenzi, and very few climb it. Those who attempt to do so must earn their laurels and must know how to climb on rock, ice and snow at altitude. The margins of error can be slim and the penalties for exceeding them dire. In 1967 a body was found at the foot of Mawenzi's north face, suspended from a rope which had caught on an overhang as the mountaineer had fallen. One can only imagine the man's last hours as he no doubt struggled to climb the unclimbable rope. A marksman had to sever the rope with a bullet to recover the body.

Deaths are rare on Kilimanjaro but some routes, especially on Mawenzi, are serious and need to be treated as such. The excellent little guide to Mount Kenya and Kilimanjaro, by Iain Allen, warns intending climbers that 'Mawenzi rock has a bad reputation which is only partly justified, but care is always needed. It is hard climbing from any side. . .'

It looks it. And sounds it. The following are quotes from Iain Allen's book, in the understated prose of the experienced mountaineer, concerning climbs on Mawenzi;

'The lower (icefall) may present some problems, especially after a heavy rainy season'; 'falling rocks may make the lower part of Oehler Gully unpleasant after mid-day, and detours out of the gully to the south, on bad rock, may be necessary. (At the bottom of this particular route, the guide book informs its readers, is a memorial plaque in honour of two climbers who met their deaths on these steep and sometimes treacherous slopes. The plaque, it says, is close to the start of the route 'but easily seen'). A memorial plaque is the last thing that most normal people would want to see as they prepare to climb Mawenzi, but then it is doubtful if mountaineers, as a breed, can be regarded as 'normal'.

Iain Allen, incidentally, was one of several outstanding climbers (others include Ian Howell, Mark Savage, Bill O'Connor, John Cleare, Dave Cheesmond and John Temple) who pioneered new routes on both Kibo and Mawenzi during the 1970s. They deserve their place in the mountain's roll of honour.

The quotes from Iain's book given above refer to one of many routes on Mawenzi's west-facing flank, the one most often seen and photographed. But the East Face is more daunting, a grim, fantastic complexity of rock with dead-end chimneys and gullies leading steeply up to bare cliffs of solid ice. This precipitous face, cut by two stupendous gorges, the Greater and Lesser Barrancos, is described in sober mountaineering terms as 'difficult and little explored'; 'almost virgin climbing ground, and owing to its difficulty of access, it is not likely to become much frequented by climbers'. It is not for nothing that it has been called the 'Eiger of Africa', and not surprising that it remained unconquered until 1964 when it was climbed by two members of the British Royal Air Force, Flight-Lt J R Edwards and Corporal W Thomson, then stationed in Nairobi.

Edwards realised that the only way to tackle the East Face was by way of the Great Barranco. This involved a near-vertical descent of well over a thousand metres which he described as 'straightforward'. While working their way to the lip of the Great Barranco the two climbers came across the wreckage of an East African Airways Dakota, which nine years earlier had crashed into the towering, cloud-obstructed South East Ridge. They noted that the point of impact was, tragically, only nine or ten metres from the ridge's summit. They had expected to find the wreckage and its pitiful human debris, but what they also found was far more unexpected and puzzling than the famous leopard of Kibo Crater. Having spent a bitterly cold night on the face, in rain and sleet, they emerged from a gully to be confronted by the skeleton of a large animal on a narrow ledge traversing a virtually sheer cliff at an altitude of about 4,800 metres. Astonished, they took a small bone with them, which was later identified as that of a buffalo.

The two men had no time to wonder how or why a buffalo had clambered to these precarious heights; they were too concerned with the precarious heights themselves. Having dismissed their porters and carrying only bare essentials, they bivouacked three nights, once at the foot of the Barranco and the remaining two times roped together on the main face. Shortly after dawn on Monday 26 October 1964 they reached the summit of Mawenzi having started the main climb 48 hours earlier. Their final ascent was made up a 230-metre ice couloir between the Nordecke and Hans Meyer peaks. Both climbers later described their ordeal as technically the most difficult and the toughest ascent they had ever tackled. For extra security they had used a double rope which, when fully extended, left the climbers about 30 metres apart. They needed it: had they fallen from certain ledges or footholds they would have plummeted through space for the best part of a thousand metres. At one point Edwards sat staring at a particular overhang for an hour wondering whether they should turn back, while his partner waited below. The tension must have set the fibres of the rope on edge.

The only person to follow in their footholds seems to have been the lone climber Fritz Lortscher, in March 1970. He passed the crashed Dakota and traversed to the upper part of the Great Barranco, where he bivouacked – astonishingly at such dehydrating altitudes – without water. Next day he climbed for fourteen-and-a-half hours, spending his second night on the crest of the ridge near Latham Peak. During his climb there were rock falls from all over the face between late morning and evening. 'One is lucky' he remarked later 'not to get hit'. Other minor irritations were poor visibility due to cloud and sharp, capricious rock which lacerated his hands and threatened to fall away, taking him with it. He found a little ice and snow among the crevices and that, presumably, helped to satisfy his thirst.

Kibo, docile in comparison with Mawenzi, can be deceptive. The nature of mountains, like that of men, can conceal dangerous flaws. Kibo's is called the Breach Wall. The Wall dates back about a hundred thousand years when a cataclysmic landslide from the summit swept away the south-west crater wall and much of the slopes below, gouging out the ravine now known as the Great Barranco and littering it with volcanic debris. The vertical precipice left by the breach might well have earned the name 'The Wall of Death' by now, were it not for the fact that few people accept its challenge. Iain Allen writes: 'This massive 1,400 metre wall is arguably the most serious mountain area on the African continent. Its great length, combined with altitude, avalanche danger, and dubious rock quality make it a very demanding undertaking'.

The Direct Route up the Wall was not climbed until 1978, when Rheinhold Messner and K. Renzler pioneered it. From the foot of the wall the route involves the ascent of an ice couloir followed by a climb up an 80 metre long icicle leading to the upper tier of the Diamond Glacier. From the head of the small glacier there is a relatively easy climb to the summit,

*Above: Descending into the Saddle from Kibo with
Mt. Mawenzi in the background.*

some 500 metres above. Messner and Renzler made the whole climb in an almost unbelievable 12 hours. Future parties are advised to 'allow at least 2 days for the ascent'. Messner admitted afterwards that it had been the hardest climb he had ever made, and it was this route which he described as being 'more serious than the North Face of the Eiger'. He knew what he was talking about. Soon after the Kibo climb he went on to conquer Everest, alone and without oxygen making him one of the greatest mountaineers of all time.

It is fascinating to wonder how Messner and Renzler would have felt if, on reaching Uhuru Point after their remarkable and perilous climb, and encumbered with crampons, pitons, ice-axes and ropes, they had encountered a small party of tourists who had just trudged to the top with the aid of walking sticks. Both parties, whatever route or risks they had taken, would have been rewarded by the 'spectacle of imposing majesty and unapproachable grandeur' which Hans Meyer described in 1889, especially if the crater and its ice-shelves had been layered with snow. In such conditions the whiteness of the snow contrasts vividly with the dark concentric walls of the inner crater and its central ashpit (named, incidentally, after Reusch) reminding walkers and climbers that they are standing at the peak of a volcano.

And of course the Christmas Pudding Mountain has attracted, as well as climbers, the inevitable adventurers, stunt artists and screw-balls. Parachutists have landed in the crater, hang-gliding enthusiasts have jumped off its rim, a party has played tiddlywinks at the summit and someone has run overnight from Loitokitok, near the foot of the mountain on the Kenyan side, to Uhuru Peak in 13 hours 20 minutes!. No doubt someone else has made love, or attempted to, in or around the crater, though in the Arctic temperatures and at that altitude the intial manoevering would have been fraught with terrible possibilities and the pillow talk afterwards brief and breathless.

Today, as many as 14,000 people a year from countries throughout the world set out to conquer the great White Mountain. Many of them will never know that they tread in some very distinguished footsteps, but all of them will have been aware of treading in some very humble ones, the footsteps of the people of the mountain, the Chagga guides and porters who cheerfully and expertly escort them. And all of them will have seen, down on the plains that sweep around *Oldoiny'oibor*, those other people who are less directly but no less romantically associated with Kilimanjaro, the Maasai. It is appropriate now to take a closer look at these 'people of the White Mountain'.

Above: *Mt. Mawenzi from the Saddle.*

Overleaf: *The snow-covered Saddle.*

People of the
White Mountain

A short history and cultural description
of the Maasai and Chagga people

Brief history of the Maasai

Kilimanjaro is one of the highest free-standing mountains in the world. Unlike the great peaks of the Himalaya or the Karakoram it rises from the plains themselves, and the best-known people of those plains are the Maasai. More has been written about them, more photographs taken of them, and perhaps more nonsense disseminated about them, than about any other tribe in Africa.

During the 19th century the Maasai were overlords of huge tracts of savannah and open thorn bush, stretching four hundred and fifty miles from north to south, from the Laikipia Plateau, west of Mount Kenya, down to the southern reaches of the Maasai Steppe, in Tanzania. Their land spanned the Rift Valley and much of the open country which borders it, from the shores of Lake Victoria to the plains below Kilimanjaro. One of the most charismatic figures in Maasai history, the *laibon* Mbatian, who prophesied the coming of people 'as white as cattle egrets' and their 'iron snake which would belch forth fire', lived for a while on the mountain's north-western slopes, at ol Molog.

Even Kilimanjaro is dwarfed by the spectacular scale of these expanses, but the east-central regions of Maasailand, home of *Il Kisongo*, one of seventeen Maasai-speaking peoples, are dominated by the White Mountain, *Oldoiny'oibor*. To its south lie the northern extremities of the Maasai Steppe, which is actually open thornbush rather than plain, but which has enough grassland to sustain the near-sacred cattle of the pastoral Maasai and the wildlife which shares their natural ranges. The plains to the north of Kilimanjaro, stretching westwards along the Kenya border towards the Great Rift Valley and beyond, are also part of Maasailand. At the foot of the mountain, just to the north of the border, lies Amboseli National Park administered by the local Maasai District Council. It is from Amboseli that so many of the photographs of Kilimanjaro, with an elephant or giraffe or a Maasai warrior among the foreground acacias, are taken.

Where did these people, who have captured the imagination of so many, who walk tall across these beautiful and boundless-seeming landscapes, apparently untouched by the drudgery and petty bureaucracies of urban life, originate? If the anthropologists are right, they are descended from the Nilotes, a people named after their homeland in the Nile basin in what is now southern Sudan. The Nilotes were a Negroid sub-race of hunter-gatherers, themselves tall and slender, who eventually turned to cultivation when the practice spread from western Africa around 3000 BC. As crop farmers they failed, and took up animal husbandry. Those who lived in less fertile areas forsook agriculture completely and discovered, or rediscovered, that grazing animals need grass which on the fragile topsoils of sub-Saharan Africa, is not necessarily a self-renewing source of energy. This meant rediscovering the freedom and the frustrations of life on the move: the cattle-herding Nilotes became migrants and moved south.

Another people, the Hamitic-speaking Cushites from north-eastern Africa, also moved south, settling in the northern highlands of East Africa in about 1000 BC and displacing many of the indigenous 'bushmen'. The Nilotes, deflected from their own path by eastward moving Bantu peoples, found themselves among the Cushites. It was love at first sight. Or at least the Cushites were absorbed into the Nilotic culture through intermarriage. The children of this union were the forbears of the Maasai, their descendants retaining the physical characteristics of the Nilotes and their language, Maa (from which, of course, they take their name) is also largely Nilotic although their culture reflects, more equitably, the Cushite influence.

Maasai folklore tells a more poetic tale of the tribe's origins. Interestingly enough, it involves a similar duality of

Opposite: Maasai warriors in fighting gear, an old print made about the time of the first ascent of Kilimanjaro.

Previous pages: Maasai herders on the Maasai Steppes with Mt. Kilimanjaro in the background.

Pride and prejudice – the prescribed lifestyle of the traditional Maasai

It goes without saying that a life-style which embraces cattle-raiding, war and spearing lions should be based on a Spartan up-bringing and, even now, the life of a traditional Maasai boy is rigorous. At the age of four or five his two lower incisors are knocked out (as are those of the girls) so that they would still be able to swallow milk in the event of lock-jaw. At this young age the boys are sent out into the bush each day, from dawn to dusk, entrusted with looking after lambs, kid goats and small calves. A little later the tops of their ear lobes are pierced, without anaesthetic, and the boys, still not seven, are expected to look after the slightly older animals. Soon afterwards, when their lower ear lobes are pierced and distended by plugs, the boys are considered capable of caring for the full-grown cattle. But the most important and painful ritual of all, usually in the boys' teens, is circumcision. It is, of course, no less painful for the girls but they, unlike the boys, are allowed to cry out without disgracing themselves or their families.

Whatever their sex, the youngsters suffer. Prior to the ceremony boys use clubs to hunt birds, and form their feathers into headdresses which they will wear when they have recovered from the circumcision. The man who circumcises the boys will usually be *Torrobo* (Ndorobo), one of the hunter-gatherers who, in the Maasai legend, shared the Garden of Eden with *II Parakwo*, ancestors of the Maasai. But the Garden of Eden must seem far away to the boy who sits on a stretched hide, arms folded across his chest and his body braced in a reclining position by a supporter, as the Ndorobo surgeon approaches.

No words are exchanged. The surgeon kneels before the boy and draws a horizontal white line in chalk across the initiate's forehead to ward off evil. He draws a similar line across the boy's penis. Then, with forefinger and thumb, he pulls the boy's foreskin forward, clear of the glans and, with a sharp blade, slices through it from right to left. The foreskin is then pulled down until the glans comes through the incision and two further cuts are made in the foreskin, at right angles to the first, leaving a flap of it hanging from the underside of the penis. The foreskin itself is seldom removed, as it is in other cultures.

After withstanding such pain, almost invariably with stoic self-control and again without anaesthetic, the prospect of being mauled in a lion hunt must have held few fears for the 'post graduate' Maasai. In the old days there would also be cattle raids and skirmishes for a junior warrior to look forward to but then, as now, the *olmurran's* life was largely one of self-indulgent leisure. After a short interim period between circumcision and warriorhood, during which the initiates wear their feathered head-dresses and are known as *olaibartani*, the new warriors form companies and live together in their own encampment, the *Imanyat* or *manyatta*. Such encampments might include hundreds of *moran*, numbers of their mothers, and the unmarried girls, the *nditos*. Feasting on bullocks, singing, dancing and uninhibited love-making compose the main curriculum at this college of pleasure.

Although the more warlike pastimes were banned during colonial times, and the carrying of the traditional buffalo hide shields prohibited, the long-bladed spears, the *moran's* most precious badge of office, were, and continue to be, carried. They are slowly disappearing in some areas of Maasailand, but it is a rare thing to see a traditional Maasai without at least a cattle stick in his hand. What one does sometimes see around the undefined borders of Maasailand where cultures tend to dissipate, are warriors wearing traditional tunics and hairstyles, their muscular bodies gleaming with fat and red ochre, but astride a Chinese 'Flying Pigeon' bicycle, spear projecting over one handlebar and a transistor

Opposite: A young warrior wearing a head dress of ostrich feathers.

Above: Three Maasai warriors with their traditional weapons of war and defence: the spear, the club and the shield.

radio hanging from the other, and wearing sandals of fluorescent plastic rather than cowhide.

Many of the 'Maasai' around the edges of Maasailand are in fact people whom the early European travellers referred to as WaKwavi. The true Maasai call them *Iloikop* (literally 'the dead ones') and to some extent despise them especially where they, the *Iloikop,* have turned to agriculture. The Kwavi (more properly the Parakuyu) were nevertheless part of mainstream Maasai life until the late 19th century when civil war disrupted northern Maasailand. The Kwavi, who were (and are) Maa speakers, came out of these wars badly and were forced to the eastern and southern fringes of the Maasai plains, many settling close to Kilimanjaro. Most Wakwavi, contrary to conventional thinking, are cattle herders like their cousins and have retained much of their previous life-style.

Maasai and Wakwavi warriors alike will almost always carry *simis* (the short stabbing swords worn at the waist in a red scabbard) and sometimes spears. These weapons are traditionally made by the Kunono, a clan of smiths, though often, in recent years, by craftsmen in Birmingham, England. It must seem strange to go home to steak and chips in the English Midlands after making spears and swords for Maasai warriors out on the East African plains, but the *ilmurrani* themselves don't tend to dwell upon life's idiosyncrasies. They have better things – their cattle or their girl friends – to think about.

Junior warriors are as vain about their appearance as any of the women, if not more so. A few months after circumcision, when the period of *olaibartani* is over, the new *moran's* head and eyebrows are shaved by his mother, a moment anticipated with pleasure by her for many years. But once the hair has grown back long enough, it becomes a warrior's crowning glory. Hours are spent coating it with ochre and animal fat, rolling strands into miniature twisted ropes and arranging these into the time-honoured coiffure, fore and aft of a parting which runs across the top of the head from ear to ear. The twisted hairs behind the parting are gathered into a pigtail, formed by binding the braids around a wooden peg.

A man's torso might be decorated with cicatrices (though these, if desired, must be done before circumcision) and will, almost always, be draped in a red or reddish orange *shuka,* usually but not always worn over one shoulder in the style of the Roman toga. Fashions change, the recent preferences among the Maasai being for red-dominated tartans and checks, and among the Parakuyu for rather drab Indonesian material in patterned greens, blues and yellows. Beaded or aromatic necklaces, earrings and cowhide sandals complete the *moran* outfit, and sometimes the warriors will tuck leaves from the *leleshwa* shrub under their armpits as a deodorant.

There are few more compelling sights in Africa than a Maasai warrior suddenly emerging from the bush, freshly groomed and adorned for some festivity. What they must have looked like when they descended upon enemies, their lion mane or ostrich feather head-dresses exaggerating their height, painted shields and knobkerries in one hand, spear in the other, thigh bells jingling and the whole company screaming and ululating with bloodlust, is not hard to imagine. For many enemies it was a persuasive argument in favour of discretion over valour.

Maasai warriors have inspired adulation as well as fear. Through western eyes they have been much romanticized in the 'noble savage' tradition, and it isn't difficult to see why. They are a good-looking people, if one accepts a tall, slender build and fine facial features as 'good-looking', and if one overlooks the fact that there are more Maasai than one might think who are quite short and cross-eyed. Very few of them, at least among the traditional plains dwellers, are fat. Striding across the plain, their *shukas* tugged out by the breeze, their ochre-red hair neatly braided and brooched back and their spears gleaming in the sun, the *olmurran* cut a considerable dash.

And their stay-at-home sweethearts, the *nditos,* are equally becoming, their trim figures loosely swathed in cloth and the fine lines of their faces enhanced by large, disc-like necklaces of brightly coloured beads. Uncircumcised – and therefore unmarried – girls do not wear the ornate, beaded earrings which are cherished by older women and warriors alike, though girls and boys often wear plugs through the lobes of their ears to distend the holes. These plugs might be whittled from wood but are just as likely, these days, to be discarded film canisters or small fruit juice cans.

But if the 'noble savage' of romantic western tradition is nowadays rarely savage, he is also sometimes less than noble. The Maasai are sometimes said to be promiscuous and it is true that the *entitos* and married women are often flirtatious and, by their own admission, adulterous, often with the chosen sweethearts of their youth. The tribe's social structure forbids the men of the warrior grades to marry until they became junior elders at around the age of thirty. As they often take additional wives at intervals throughout their lives, usually in ratio to the number of cattle they come to own, and as they prefer younger women, relatively old men can have wives who are little more than girls. For whatever reasons, the girls, like the men, often 'stray'. If discovered they can usually expect a beating – wife-beating is common among the Maasai, as it is among other tribes. Most women seem to accept this philosophically, even with good-humoured resignation, but drunkenness is another common problem among the Maasai and the treatment of wives can sometimes be brutal.

It doesn't stop many women from smiling readily at warriors and strangers alike, and their smiles are sweet enough to seduce a saint. Or depress a dentist. The Maasai generally have beautiful white teeth, as one might expect from a diet based on milk. Nor do the Maasai, male or female, have too many sexual hang-ups. Children learn young, and junior *moran* commonly consort with pre-pubescent girls in their *Imanyat* or *manyatta* – the 'warrior camp'. Because of the girls' immaturity pregnancies are rare, but if an *entito* does become pregnant, she has two alternatives; abortion by means of certain herbs or, as soon as possible, clitoridectomy – the removal of the clitoris and part of the labia minor which, in traditional Maasai society, must be carried out before marriage.

No stigma is attached to such 'accidents of nature' as might be the case in the west. Maasai society is, in many respects, more enlightened than that of many so-called 'civilised' peoples and, perhaps, a good deal less neurotic. Stress is common to all societies and the Maasai are no exception but on the whole, despite such problems as the foregoing mentions, they are – or appear to be – a happy and contented community, with a well-defined but liberal way of life. Unlike many tribes they do not have a paramount chief, and authority is vested in the tribal elders and various democratically elected leaders such as the *Olaiguenani,* or Chief Councillor, who controls his age-set from his election (preceding circumcision) through to death or serious disability. All of these men (Maasai society is very much male-orientated) are accorded great respect.

Maasai justice and morality is based on tolerance and a broad-minded view of life. Penalties for many crimes are restricted to fines, not of money but of the 'coin of the realm' – cattle, sheep or goats. Even murder, in the old days, was

Above: Elegantly decorated with ruffs and necklace,
this ten-year-old girl is already wise about life
among the moran in the manyatta where they live.

Opposite: Illmurrani, *dancing the* adumu, *the bouncing, jumping dance in which the men compete to jump highest while singing. To perform during the* eunoto, *their graduation ceremony at which they officially become junior warriors.*

Below: *Moran fires an arrow into an ox's jugular. The spurting blood gushes into a gourd. Later, mixed with milk, it becomes a protein-rich 'Maasai cocktail' - a ritual drink for special celebrations and for the sick who need nourishment.*

only punished by death in the heat of the moment. More often than not the murderer was hidden away until tempers cooled, and a large fine imposed. This fine might have been forty-nine cows or two hundred and forty-nine sheep, but the number nine was important, being the number of orifices in a man's body. Why the number of orifices in a man's body was the determining factor is unclear, but the fact that the male body was specified probably reflects the sex of the murder victim. The Maasai code of honour precluded the killing of women, those women of enemy tribes.

Domestic life is also regulated with magnanimity and open-mindedness. Divorce is not unknown and a wife will sometimes leave her husband to live with another man. In such a case she will forfeit certain rights but there is no ostracism or lasting bad feeling. Wives who remain with their husbands are in theory, and often in practice, available to their husbands age-set, the group of men who were circumcised at the same time. The choice, however, is the woman's and she can say no to any of them at any time. A wife often has to share her husband (who might be much older than her) with other wives, but on the other hand unmarried older women are unknown in Maasai society, and loneliness rare.

Life for all Maasai women, as with many African tribes, is hard. Apart from enduring the horrors of clitoridectomy and its gruesome aftermath, having to please husbands who are not always sober or gentle, and sharing their man with several other women, they are expected to milk the cows, look after babies, kids and lambs, act as butcher for children and elders (no woman is allowed to touch or even set eyes upon meat intended for warriors), tan hides and tailor clothes. They are carriers of babies, collectors of firewood, and bearers of water. During the rains, when most of the inhabitants of the *enkang* disperse with their herds, it is the women who load those other beasts of burden, the donkeys, with household possessions, and who accompany them to the temporary encampments out among the fresh green pasture. Women, quite literally, are also homemakers and build, out of leafy *leleshwa* branches which are unattractive to termites, the low, loaf-like huts which are plastered with a waterproof coating of cow dung.

The huts of an *enkang* are placed in a circle and the position of each hut is significant, reflecting the status of family members. Each hut has three sections. A square-spiralled entrance leads around (and sometimes through) a narrow room, completely or partly walled off from the other two rooms by a screen of stripped *leleshwa* stems. This room or 'hallway' is in fact used as a stable for calves, kids or lambs at night, a practice for non-Maasai guests to be aware of should they stay overnight in an *enkang*. The main room of the hut is a living-room, bedroom and kitchen all in one. The bed itself is a low structure fashioned from poles and covered with cow hides, used for seating family members and guests in the day time and as a bed (often a communal one) by night. If the man of the family has only one wife he will use this bed regularly – otherwise he divides his time and sometimes his energies more or less equally among the other women in his life.

Facing this room will normally be the wife's private room, walled off, like the stabling enclosure, by a screen of *leleshwa*. It will contain a small bed, used by the woman and her youngest children when her husband is not a at home or when guests are using the 'master bedroom'. Stowed away among the recesses in the wall behind the bed, or elsewhere in the room, will be pots and pans and gourds, supplies of milk or honey beer, and the woman's personal possessions. These will be few and simple; plastic or ceramic beads, cowrie shells (symbols of fertility and much prized) and other ornamental objects all contained, as a rule, in a small, beaded leather bag. This bag and its contents are as dear to a Maasai woman as any western woman's jewellery box.

Above: An aerial view of a Maasai homestead.

The Maasai, both young and old, are dedicated to the welfare of their herds.

The women are helped in their household chores and milking by the girls, while the boys are out in the bush tending their fathers' bank-account-on-the-hoof. Despite these early responsibilities Maasai children have fun. They enjoy themselves most when the working day ends, and anyone who has witnessed the simple pleasure of an evening in a Maasai *enkang* will have few fears for the well-being of the children. They run and jump and chase each other around the enclosure, play games with bits of charcoal and listen to their elders telling stories or proverbs. Like African children in general, they are treasured by adults, young and old alike, and treated with affection. One of the most moving sights in the catalogue of human relationships is to see Maasai children approaching an elder one by one, head bowed to receive the old man's blessing, as he gently lays a hand upon each lowered head. It is a gesture full of love and respect and natural grace, a beautiful silent tribute to a community at peace with itself, and with the land.

Old people themselves are not only respected but cared for. A very old man becomes a *Desati*, an ancient retired elder. At this stage his social responsibilities end, but the community provides for him until death. Old women are cared for, in a similar manner, by their youngest son. When death brings the final stage of Maasai life to a close, only distinguished elders and the Maasai seers and oracles, the *laibon*, are buried. The bodies of less elevated mortals are put out in the bush, their remains eaten by creatures great or small – often hyenas. To western minds this might seem callous, but what better grave could a Maasai wish for than to lie under the sun and stars, amid the grass which has nurtured his beloved cattle, and which in turn will be nurtured by the salts of his body.

It is impossible to understand the Maasai without understanding the importance of grass. The roots of the grasses which flourish with the rain across Maasailand are at the roots of Maasai life. Drawing moisture and minerals from the earth, usually, as around Kilimanjaro, from the rich volcanic topsoils, the grasses feed the lifeblood of the cows which feed the lifeblood of their doting masters. It is the search for more nutritious grass which leads the Maasai on, not to pastures new, for the Maasai are not by nature nomads, but to pastures fresh. The Maasai, like so much of the wildlife which shares their lands, move back and forth with the rains coming and going twice a year, dependent only on good grazing, water and the will of God.

The Maasai, of course, live on processed grass. Their diet is almost exclusively confined to milk and occasionally meat (the milk sometimes supplemented by blood from a living cow, but no longer as often as some writers have implied). Grass has a ceremonial significance too, because of its direct association with cattle. The Maasai believe that when *Engai* presented them with cattle he used the long aerial roots of the wild fig tree as a conduit. Whenever the pastoralists encounter such a fig tree they will honour God, and the tree itself, by placing a handful of grass among the hanging roots. During certain ceremonies, such as circumcision, important participants, such as the fathers of boys being circumcised, will carry gourds stoppered with a plug of grass. And grass was used in the past as a token of peace. When faced with strangers of a different clan, individuals would pluck a tuft of grass and hold it in their outstretched hands to announce their peaceful intent. Soon after death, at least for those important enough to be buried, a clump of grass is placed in one hand of the corpse. None of us knows what awaits beyond the grave, and a token of peace is perhaps a prudent insurance policy.

Brief history of the Chagga

If we cannot begin to understand the Maasai without understanding their dependence upon grass, then we cannot begin to understand one of their traditional enemies, the Chagga, without understanding the importance, to them, of Kilimanjaro. The mountain gives them shelter and sustenance but above all an identity, an old, precise, deep-rooted sense of place.

The mountain also gives the Chagga a sense of unity: Kilimanjaro is where they belong. It represents home, and history, and reassurance against an uncertain future. Few other African peoples have such a clear focal point with which to identify. Those of us who are spared the tyranny of endless horizons, where the bush or the grass sweeps unremittingly on and on, as if for ever, must not underestimate the power of a mountain which rises, with such massive self-assurance, from the unassertive African plain.

Whatever influence the mountain exerts, the Chagga are a race apart. They tend to hold, and invite, strong views. They are known, by their admirers, for their intelligence and enterprise and, by their detractors, for their ruthlessly sharp practices. The Chagga, not given to much introspection, don't seem to care one way or the other. They just get on with life, and with business. With their coffee estates on and around Kilimanjaro and their varied enterprises throughout Tanzania, they are important contributors to the country's economy, and to its cultural vitality. It is curious that they have so often been overlooked by the outside world, and relatively neglected even by people writing about their homeland, Kilimanjaro.

This is unfortunate. The Chagga, to a tourist or expatriate, might not be as romantic or as spectacular as the Maasai, but they are an intriguing people with a long and interesting past and it is they, far more than the pastoralists of the surrounding plains, who are the true people of the great White Mountain. They actually inhabit the Kilimanjaro foothills on all but its northerly slopes, right up to the boundaries of the Kilimanjaro National Park which encircle the two peaks along the lower reaches of the rainforest. And they provide the guides and porters who slog up and down the mountain, taking care of the hundreds of thousands of travellers and tourists who attempt the long trek to the highest point in Africa.

Unlike the Maasai, the Chagga are Bantu, many of whom are thought to have filtered through into East Africa from the Congo Basin area around AD 1300. Some anthropologists believe that they eventually came to Kilimanjaro from the Taita Hills, a hundred kilometres or so to the east. Others think that they came from the north-east. Similar but smaller migrations from the south, of people driving others north or being driven themselves, might have taken place. From wherever they came, their signpost in the sky was Kilimanjaro. Whether they were forced to retreat into its steep forests and high plateaus by the marauding Maasai (as some Chagga will tell you), or were drawn by the climate and the well-watered, fertile soils is difficult to determine. The truth perhaps embraces both possibilities.

But come they did, and Kilimanjaro became to the Chagga what the high grasslands were to the Maasai, their natural home. Oral traditions of the Chagga suggest that Kilimanjaro was unpopulated until about 1500 AD, and that no significant migrations into the area took place until the 18th century. More scientific research implies that the lower slopes of Kilimanjaro have been continuously occupied for two thousand years or more: that the Chagga and their Bantu counterparts had been settled in the area long before the 1500s, and that in subsequent centuries other immigrants arrived, from places such as the Taita Hills and the Maasai plains.

Opposite: A 19th-century woodcut of a Chagga village on the slopes of Kilimanjaro.

'Sultan of Moshi' (the Islamic connotation was no accident – Rindi always encouraged the caravans from the coast, trading slaves and ivory for cloth, and later guns. He even taught himself fluent Swahili). In 1862 von der Decken was welcomed to Moshi by the 'handsome' young chief and his dominating, doting mother who spoke on his behalf. But the 'Mummy's boy' grew up, as later explorers and missionaries were to discover.

Twenty years after von der Decken's visits Joseph Thomson encountered the then famous chief. The Scot didn't exactly confirm the chief's self-image as 'the cloud that overshadows all lands'. 'Chagga', he observes, 'is all broken up into a number of small states which would hardly make a gentleman's estate in (Britain). The inhabitants, however, fight like bull-dogs for hearth and home, and are incessantly at war with each other. There is absolutely no intercourse, and it is war to the knife whenever they meet. Mandara, the most noted of all the warrior chiefs, has long had imperial views, and has murdered and devastated hard to carry them into effect; but though he has, time after time, laid waste the neighbouring states, he has as yet reduced none to submission, though many to starvation, so tenaciously do they stick to their districts and mountain freedom'.

Chagga chiefs were known for their cupidity. Rebmann had been reduced to tears by chiefs Masaki and Mamkinga, who robbed the poor and gentle missionary of all his barter goods, forcing him to abandon his expedition. He returned to the coast a sick and embittered man, never again to travel to the mountain he had 'discovered', or into the interior, though he remained in East Africa for another twenty-six years.

Mangi Rindi (Mandara) maintained the tradition. On his first meeting with Thomson the chief could hardly take his eye (he only had one) off the Scot's fine safari boots. Between bouts of quaffing beer and spitting Rindi whistled in wonder at the excellence of the explorer's footwear. He didn't actually demand anything until some days later, when his monocular gaze focused on Thomson's guns and scientific instruments.

One of these instruments, the galvanometer, threw Rindi 'into fits of astonishment. His eagle eye gleamed with covetousness and he spat and whistled himself dry, requiring incessant libations of *pombe* to sustain him. He intensely enjoyed ordering his chiefs and warriors to submit to the electric current, and he simply gloated over their evident though suppressed terror, while they with difficulty kept themselves from yelling out or wriggling on the ground'. Rindi himself declined the ordeal because, Thomson assumed, he was afraid of being bewitched. In fact the chief, as Thomson acknowledged, was an impressive and intelligent man who didn't need a degree in physics to know that his warriors were hardly writhing around in ecstasy.

Rindi's acquisitiveness, however, had been aroused, and Thomson felt obliged to present the chief with a few gifts, including a rifle, a revolver and some colourful cloths. Rindi's eye screwed itself into an expression of contempt. 'Are these', he asked, 'the presents for my *askari?*' (his one-man bodyguard). Without waiting for an answer he stormed off in a chiefly huff, later issuing vague but menacing threats against the explorer and his party. Thomson took the warnings seriously, and spent the next morning mending his fences with Rindi, a peace process expedited by the surrendering, among other items, of Thomson's tweed suit and a pair of shoes.

The missionary Charles New had been similarly treated by Rindi. Even Harry Johnston, who got on with the chief better than many others, had his differences with the temperamental Chagga leader. But the Chagga were not the only

Opposite: Memorial plaque, at the Marangu gate entrance, dedicated to the porters who accompanied Hans Meyer to the summit.

YOHANA LAUWO

MTANZANIA WA KWANZA KUMFIKISHA
MPANDAJI WA KWANZA KILELENI
KILIMANJARO 1889

Lin. ..kumbu kumbu za wenu walioongoze

..anda. mlima wa kwanza.

————————————— * ——————— * —————

This plaque commemorates the first guides
and porters who assisted the first climbers to
reach the summit of Mt. Kilimanjaro on 6-10-1889.

1. Yohana Lauwo —— Guide.

2. Jonathan Mtui —— Asst. Guide.

3. Elia Minja —— Porter.

4. Toma Mosha —— Porter.

5. Makelio Lyimo —— Porter.

6. Mamba Kowera —— Porter.

African tribe to practice extortion, and the Europeans, Arabs and other outsiders were not usually in any position to moralise. The Chagga could certainly be aggressive and greedy (there are many who would say they still are) but they could also be welcoming and open-handed. Thomson was impressed by Mandara's 'evident intelligence' and 'lavish hospitality', and the chief and short-sword 'splendid specimens of Wa-chaga workmanship'. This generous side to Rindi's nature was confirmed by other European visitors.

And if the Chagga were sometimes unpleasant towards outsiders they could be just as nasty to each other. The southern slopes of Kilimanjaro, so benign and beautiful to today's tourists, were nourished with blood as well as water. Tales of slaughter and murder are commonplace. Thomson talks of Rindi 'carrying out his' imperial views' with the usual course of murder and devastation', and Rindi, it seemed, was determined to rule the whole south-west corner of Chaggaland.

But he was a diplomat rather than a general (though the British monarch Victoria might not have agreed – he referred to her Imperial Highness as 'Queenie'). Nevertheless, he and his men had to be prepared for war. An etching in Thomson's *Through Masai Land* shows three of Rindi's warriors who might easily have been taken for Maasai *moran*, and the Scot confirms that the Chagga 'affect the weapons of the Maasai – namely, great shovel-headed spears, the *sime*, knobkerry, and the large elliptically shaped buffalo-hide shield ornamented with an heraldic device in colours. These were all beautiful specimens of native workmanship, the Wa-chaga of Moschi being quite unrivalled as blacksmiths in Africa'.

The Chagga's mountain strongholds (or at least their chiefs' quarters) were well fortified. Mangi Rindi's personal residence was of quadrangular Swahili style plastered with dung and clay, but his fifty or more wives were housed in traditional bee-hive huts. This inner sanctum, which was surrounded by a triple pallisade of massive tree trunks, also housed domestic stock. Outside stood eight large huts, each containing seven or eight young women. These girls would eventually be sold into slavery or given 'as rewards to the soldiers for services done'. There were plenty of soldiers looking for such bounty. One hundred warriors kept a nightly watch upon the compound, 'ever ready to raise the war-cry, and rush upon all intruders' (and, given half a chance, no doubt, to rush upon the sixty-odd damsels).

The soldiers might have lusted after the girls but the young and roving eye of Joseph Thomson was not much taken with them: 'When the moon is bright, and the chief's spirits high', he writes, 'these damsels dance on the dewy grass, waking the echoes of the neighbouring glens with their wierd, ear-piercing screams, and looking like witches in the ruddy glare of the bonfires'. What the girls thought of the pasty-faced Thomson remains – unfortunately – unrecorded.

War on Kilimanjaro was as dirty as it is anywhere else. One particular atrocity, perpetrated by Chief Rengua of Machame in the early 19th century, is still remembered on Kilimanjaro and is said to be still capable of making men weep. Rengua's warriors slaughtered a group of Kibosho initiates who were recovering, by a sacred swamp, from the ordeal of their recent circumcision. The murder of relatively helpless men, during the most important ritual of their young lives, represented a breach of trust and tribal etiquette so shameful that Machame people still prefer not to discuss it. In Kibosho it is remembered in songs of sadness.

The Machame cannot be proud, either, of another of their former chieftains, Mangi Ndesserua. Von der Decken, in 1861, described him as 'a strong young man of about 20 years with a big fat nose, plaited hair and the eyes of a drunkard', much feared for his wicked temper. It is said that he forced his warriors to eat meat mixed with the blood of his murdered victims, but he is also remembered for giving away bananas and beer to his people. He was, however, prone to assassinate even the people he 'liked', and so much feared that relatives of men he had murdered would thank him with a gift.

Tyrants rarely suffer poetic justice but the fat-nosed Ndesserua was an exception. His mid-life crisis was compounded by an affliction which caused him to shrivel into a deformed dwarf, crippled and unable to move, his toe and finger nails 'as long as leopards claws'. But his evil mind remained active and the killings went on, at the hands of his subordinates. Fate caught up with him again, however, when his chiefdom was raided by the Arush. The Machame warriors who survived ran away, carrying their deformed chief who died, lonely and unmourned, soon afterwards.

In Kibosho, to the east, another new chief, Mangi Sina, had come to power. Kathleen Stahl rates him as 'the greatest warrior chief Kilimanjaro was ever to know'. He was certainly one of the most effective – and most ruthless. Right from the start he killed off opponents within Kibosho itself, and frightened most of the rest into submission or exile. He then sent his warriors out to raid and plunder the neighbouring states. All these raids, and all subsequent ones, were successful, a unique achievement on Kilimanjaro and a tribute to his masterful military acumen.

He built his headquarters on a high promontory formed by a loop in the river Kyumbara. At its centre was a massive fortress, humming with activity. Bodyguards worked round the clock and his warriors, hand-picked for their fearlessness, lived in barracks around the outside of the walls. And like all good armies Sina's marched on its stomach. Ten to twenty cows were killed each day to feed it, and the beef was washed down with banana beer. Up to a thousand men queued for their daily ration. His wives lived within the walls in bee-hive huts, and close by lived expert blacksmiths. They were tied to their job – quite literally, being chained by the legs.

Beyond the fortress, Sina's people were relatively well treated. He was a dictator, but a relatively benevolent one. He treated his subjects as slaves, and enjoyed access to any of the women, but he is remembered for his paternal generosity. He fed and clothed his people as best he could and under him his country, which had previously suffered famine, became green with bananas and waving fields of eleusine. Hans Meyer, conqueror of Kibo, called Kibosho the 'real Promised Land of Kilimanjaro'.

It was an impressive set-up, and it worked. Sina made Kibosho the most powerful territory on Kilimanjaro. He avenged the slaughter of the Kibosho initiates, attacking Machame and razing it to the ground. And his tactics could be creative. To fool enemy agents into thinking that he was terminally ill, he took to wearing a bull's scrotum around his own (which says something about his fortitude as well as his inventiveness). Not surprisingly this unusual underwear gave off a pretty ripe stench, suggesting that the chief was moribund.

Rumours of his eventual death were very much exaggerated. His warriors were sent off into enemy territory to spread the disinformation, and the enemy warriors (from Machame) were invited back to Kibosho, ostensibly to make peace and to help choose a new chief. In the meantime the enterprising (and very-much-alive) Sina stuck a decomposing goat's carcase in his otherwise empty hut to further convince the gullible Machame that he was, in fact, dead. The Machame were apparently fooled, and of course massacred.

The Chagga in German times

Sina's tricks didn't fool the Germans, who later began to colonise the area. Suspicious of the chief's loyalties, they attacked his fortress in a battle which stands out as the mountain's military epic. Both sides fought with guns and spears, but for the first time a machine gun, the deadly Maxim, was used on Kilimanjaro. The Kibosho warriors had no answer to it but they displayed tremendous courage, and Sina's fortress was only taken at comparatively heavy cost.

Sina surrendered and lived for six more years, retaining considerable power. He was, however, watched by a German agent and further threatened from a most unlikely source, a Roman Catholic missionary called Father Rohmer. The Holy Father had a most unholy temper and a mighty build to back it up (the Chagga called him 'The Wild Pig'). His sacred duties did not, it appears, extend to diplomacy, and he treated the once-great Sina with contempt. On one occasion, when refused entry into Sina's hut, 'The Wild Pig' ordered the chief (in a voice which could be heard, it was said, a mile away) to show his 'ugly face'. Sina (who could blame him?) stayed put, whereupon Rohmer smashed down the door with a massive boulder, almost killing the terrified occupants.

Rohmer had Germany as well as God on his side and Sina was relatively helpless. The 'Scramble for Africa' was well under way, with an increasing German presence on the mountain. In 1886 the British and Germans had drawn a line on a map which determined the common border between their two new colonies. The kink in that otherwise straight line had decided, at a stroke, the political fate of Kilimanjaro and the Chagga, for it left both the mountain and the tribe under German control, and explains why they remain in Tanzania today, rather than Kenya.

The Germans were widely regarded as harsh rulers. But they did much to develop the area, introducing economic, educational and social practices which the Chagga were quick to absorb. The Germans also brought in experts in medicine, agriculture, geology and botany. The British, when they took over in 1916, were more easy-going but more neglectful, perhaps, of their developmental obligations. Meanwhile the Chagga learned to live (and sometimes die) with both regimes, and to learn from each of them.

The Chagga chiefs were threatened from within as well as without. Sina survived the German onslaught of his fort only to fall to an enemy who worked in much subtler ways. On the day of Pentecost, 1897, ironically with his people celebrating Mass in Rohmer's mission, Sina died suddenly of 'stomach trouble' which, in Chaggaland at the time, suggested something more sinister than bad bananas. The man behind Sina's terminal tummy-ache was widely believed to have been a chief whom Sina had helped to instal, and whom he regarded as almost like a nephew', Mangi Marealle of Marangu.

Whether Marealle (the anglicized form of Melyari) poisoned his former patron or not will never be proved. But he was undoubtedly capable of it. An opportunist and a schemer, his manipulation of people and events secured his reputation as a politician par excellence. But he was also imaginative and bold, and a man of vision. His story was almost a classical tale of rags to riches and as his own fortunes rose, so too did those of the chiefdom of Marangu. He transformed it from an almost destitute region to a territory of distinction and influence.

He didn't do it by force of arms (he only accompanied his warriors on one raid from which he had to be hustled off to safety). But what he lacked in valour he made up for by a genuine charm, at least towards friends and guests, and a

Opposite: The cover of Hans Meyer's book about his first ascent in German language.

rather dramatic presence. When Count Teleki and von Höhnel attempted to climb Kilimanjaro in 1887 they made Marangu their base camp, as have so many climbers since. Teleki found himself confronted by a young man (Marealle was twenty-seven) who claimed to be a hundred and who wore a pencil-like stick through one ear, a 'wooden plug the size of a saucer' through the other and an American general's red coat. The coat was trimmed with gold braid and embellished with the skins of black-and-white colobus monkeys and the feathers of vultures.

This daring wardrobe was made more so by the acquisition from Teleki, of a gilded dragoon's helmet. The effects of all this on subjects and visitors alike is sadly unrecorded. What is recorded is that Marealle had, like Rindi of Moshi, an eye for the main chance, alleviated by a similar generosity and hospitality towards European guests. Rindi became immensely jealous of his younger rival's diplomatic successes, and the rising prestige that went with them. Until 1891, when Rindi died, Marealle had to keep a wary eye on the chiefdom a little way to the west and, in fact, Marangu was raided by Moshi as late as 1889.

But Marealle was a survivor. And, even by the scheming standards of the time, a Machiavelli of the White Mountain. He soon found a like-minded partner. In 1891 he met the notorious Carl Peters who, until he was sent home in disgrace, spent some months as officer in charge of Kilimanjaro. Peters was the first of the Germans to make Marangu his headquarters and, to pass the lonely mountain nights more congenially, he took one of the youngest and prettiest of Marealle's wives, Ndekocha, as his mistress, presumably with the chief's approval. The girl soon ran away, into the arms of Chief Malamya of Mamba. Marealle has been accused of ordering her defection in order to discredit Malamya and if so, it says much about Marealle's moralities. With characteristic callousness Peters deposed Malamya and hanged the girl from a roadside tree by the River Una, a spot tourists pass when approaching the Kibo Hotel.

Ndekocha was not the only person to be hung because of the alleged involvement of Marealle. In 1900 a supposed conspiracy against the Germans was savagely suppressed by them and their Chagga levies. The two main 'conspirators', Molelia and Meli, young chieftains of Kibosho and Moshi respectively, were arrested together with 17 of their supporters. The next day they 'confessed' and on the following morning were hung, one by one, from a tree outside the German *Boma* in Old Moshi. Meli, son of Mangi Rindi, sang a song before climbing, unaided, the natural gallows. He took so long to die that in the end he had to be shot.

The Chagga of the 20th century

Throughout his career Marealle cleverly used his personal charm to advantage, especially with the Europeans. But soon after the hangings in Moshi, he himself was accused of plotting, with the Maasai, to overthrow the German authorities. Fearing for his life he fled in 1904 to Nairobi. He later returned and was reinstated but retired in 1912 to live in the hut of his youngest wife, the only one (of between fifty and a hundred) who could be bothered to feed him. He died in 1916.

In that same year, working in the same *Boma* in Old Moshi which the Germans had recently vacated, a Chagga interpreter named Merinyo fell in love with a lady by the name of Ruth Fisha, the estranged wife of a chief. Her unromantic name belied a romantic past. As a young girl she had been presented, together with an elephant tusk tied with near-sacred *masale* leaves, to the great Mangi Sina, as a peace offering. Now she was to become, through her lover's influence and the backing of the new British administration, the mother of one of the last great chiefs of the Chagga, Mangi Abdiel Shangali.

Abdiel was installed at the age of 20 and was to rule until 1946. He was a commanding man, blessed with outstanding personal qualities and like so many Chagga chiefs before him, he was also a shrewd politician, said 'to love power more consistently than any other Chagga had ever done'. Which is saying something. He quickly gained an understanding of the new overlords of Kilimanjaro, the British, and used them to bolster his own situation and that of his chiefdom, Machame.

The British administrators, well versed in the tactics of indirect rule, found Abdiel to their liking. The Chagga themselves, even Abdiel's own people, saw him in a different light. His style of government was often uncompromising and the atmosphere in Machame tense and, despite every effort by the British the Chagga refused to accept Abdiel as their paramount chief. Yet his achievements were remarkable. His personal empire covered half of lower Kilimanjaro and he became not only the most powerful hereditary chief of the whole period of British rule, but also the most illustrious leader in the history of his region. Not least of his achievements was the economic improvements he brought about, largely through urging his people to plant coffee.

Another important Chagga leader of the twentieth century, and in fact the Chagga's last Paramount Chief, was Mangi Thomas Marealle who, at the time of writing, is a little frail but very much alive. The grandson of Mangi Marealle I, his rather more audacious and ruthless ancestor, Thomas is interesting in his own right. He was known as 'King Tom' and the regal title was not altogether inappropriate for he was invited to Queen Elizabeth II's coronation, and helped to escort the monarch when she visited Tanzania and Kilimanjaro years later.

A sepia photograph of his investiture shows the chief in traditional regalia with a leopard skin cloak surmounted by a cape of colobus fur. Around his neck hangs a broad, beaded necklace from which hangs a large diamond-shaped pendant as he bows slightly forward to be fitted with an ornate ceremonial cap, a little like a bishop's mitre. The uniform recalls the eccentric tastes of his grandfather but any temptations, on the part of we outsiders to smirk, would be foolish, for the British governor who is pictured fitting the hat on to Thomas's handsome head looks at least twice as absurd in his own ceremonial regalia.

Thomas had – and has – style. The English satirist Evelyn Waugh met him in the late 1950s and described him as 'an

Opposite: A Chagga porter standing on the summit of Uhuru peak.

85

to the spirit of the unborn child, in case it actually belongs to some long forgotten ancestor. Goats (or among poorer families, chickens) are sacrificed and curious neighbours are banned from the hut where the woman is confined, for fear that out of jealousy or spite, they might cast the evil eye upon the foetus, or work mischief through witchcraft, magic or poison. The mother might remain secluded in the hut for almost three months after the birth.

Compared with the Maasai, the Chagga had a narrower outlook with regard to sex and marriage and, in the past, would destroy illegitimate or deformed children at birth. Marriages without parental approval would be (and sometimes still are) blighted with the curse of childlessness and children, born or unborn, receive the attentions of all the extended family's adults; the successful production and upbringing of children is too serious a matter to be left to the parents, married or otherwise.

Life for most Chagga children is neither easy nor particularly harsh. Most of them are sent to one of the many small schools on the mountain and on the whole they learn quickly and well. They are, like their Maasai counterparts, expected to help around the house at times, or with the livestock, but education takes priority and successful students, male or female, are not expected to sacrifice careers in business or commerce for more traditional pursuits. Laziness is frowned upon in Chagga society generally, and great pressure is brought to bear upon youngsters who don't work hard – another reason why the tribe is so advanced and successful.

Chagga boys are circumcised, but under hygenic medical conditions and girls are spared the shocking mutilations of clitoridectomy. After school or university many young Chagga will leave their beloved Kilimanjaro, often for months or years at a time, to put their talents and expertise to good use elsewhere in Tanzania or East Africa, or, if fortune has favoured them, in lands beyond the sea. But no matter how far the Chagga wander, the great white mountain calls them back. For those returning by air, the sight of that snow-clad peak must bring a few tears to eyes yearning for a glimpse of home.

For those who stay in Chaggaland, by choice or by circumstance, life is far from unpleasant. Money might not be easy to come by and the life-style might be simple, even exacting, but the air is cool and healthy and the land, tended and tilled by numberless generations, looks after its own. Bananas are plentiful and cheap and so are maize, millet and milk while king coffee makes money sometimes, for some. Above all, the Chagga have their mountain which gives them not only water but peace of mind reassures them, day after day and year after year, of their identity: of their treasured links with the past and with their revered ancestors.

And when the time comes for a Chagga to join those ancestors more literally, it is under that volcanic soil that they wish to be buried. Families will do their utmost to bring a dead or dying Chagga back home from whichever corner of the world. And home means only one thing – the mountain. Which Chagga, in death, would choose to be buried elsewhere? And in life, which Chagga could feel isolated, rootless or cut off from his culture when he or she can see, above the fickle clouds, the unchanging, blue-grey bulk of Kilimanjaro?

Above: The western slopes of the mountain are perfect for farming wheat.

Folk Tales of Kilimanjaro

Why Kibo And Mawenzi Were Separated

As one might expect, the Chagga have several folk tales featuring the mountain which dominates their lives. When viewed from the Saddle, the difference between the mountain's two main peaks, twelve kilometres apart, makes it easier for us to understand why the Chagga have no name for the whole massif, only for the peaks themselves – *Kipoo* and *Kimawenzi*. This perception of the mountain as two rather than one is implicit in the following folk story, which tells how Kibo and Mawenzi became separated.

A poor man called Mlai once set off to the far side of Kibo to look for cattle. He met an old woman who helped and directed him, and soon came upon a great herd. But the cattle would not follow him. He returned to the old lady and asked for help. She gave him a staff and said 'Drive an ox with this, and the rest will follow'. Her strategy worked, but only until the hapless Mlai and his newly acquired herd reached Kibo and Mawenzi, which in legendary days were side by side. Kibo refused to let them pass and Mlai, once again, sought help. The old woman (who by this time must have doubted the man's ability to take charge of a tin of corned beef, let alone a herd of intransigent cattle) promised Mlai that if he would help her plough her fields she would solve his latest problem. Mlai agreed and, on completion of the ploughing, was given some magic powder, wrapped up in (what else?) a banana leaf. He was commanded to go back and blow the powder against the rocks of Kibo, which he did with dramatic effect. Immediately the two peaks were split asunder, coming to rest where they now stand. Mlai drove his cattle across the newly formed Saddle and down through the forest until he eventually reached home. Behind every great man – and a lot of helpless ones – is a great woman.

Why Mawenzi Looks so rugged compared with Kibo

If another Chagga folk tale is to be believed, Mawenzi's brooding isolation and craggy features become understandable. In ancient times, when Kibo and Mawenzi were sitting by their respective hearths, Mawenzi allowed his fire to go out. He approached his bigger but younger brother to ask for a few embers. Kibo complied, and, being a good Chagga, gave him one or two bananas, to see him back across the Saddle. Perhaps preoccupied with the bananas, poor Mawenzi let the coals go out again, and went back to replenish them. Kibo gave him more embers and more bananas but, before long Mawenzi returned for the third time, overestimating, as so many brothers do, the limits of fraternal affection. Kibo, unamused, picked up a club and beat his younger brother so badly that his features were drastically rearranged. Which was, even for mighty volcanoes, something of an over-reaction. Now Mawenzi sulks across the Saddle bemoaning the unfairness of life and the barbaric nature of younger brothers. And looking rather the worse for wear.

Kilimanjaro's Elephant Graveyard

Mawenzi is not alone in his sufferings. Elephants have been persecuted for centuries throughout Africa and those on Kilimanjaro are no exception. The Chagga have their own version of the well-known myth regarding an elephants' graveyard, somewhat modified to fit the unusual topographical circumstances. The Chagga interpretation speaks of a pit high on Kibo (the ash pit at the crater?) into which dying elephants hurl themselves to thwart the poachers and ivory hunters. The Chagga, however, being natural business people, allow for a little opportunism in their legends; any man who dares to climb down into the pit can help himself to a piece of ivory as long as greed doesn't get the better of him. Those grubbing around for the biggest tusks are immediately struck blind, before meeting a wretched death at the bottom of the pit (the nature of this death is unspecified but one might assume that it isn't too pleasant).

King Menelik and the Treasures of King Solomon

One final story concerns treasures of a different kind, and owes its origins to a very different people from a more distant land. It connects Kilimanjaro with the first king of Abyssinia, Menelik I, son of Solomon and Sheba, who governed the old province of Tigre as *Negusi-Negeshti* , King of Kings.

The legend assures us that Menelik, returning with spoils of war from a journey of conquest, camped on the Saddle between Kibo and Mawenzi. He was apparently wanting in the wisdom for which his illustrious father was famous, for to climb unnecessarily to the Saddle and camp there is not the wisest thing to do, especially as Menelik was 'old and tired of life and felt death drawing near'. But kings are often better known for pride rather than prudence, and perhaps he was stubbornly fulfilling a death wish. 'King I am', he announced to his followers, 'and as a king I wish to die'.

Death wishes are fairly easy to realise on Kilimanjaro and Menelik, to give him credit, went out in style. One morning he bid farewell to his army and, accompanied by a few war lords, set off for the summit. They were accompanied by a train of slaves, each carrying jewels and treasure. The soldiers waiting below watched as their king and his entourage reached the snow-line and were lost to view among the clouds. In the evening the War Lords returned (thankfully, it might be imagined). Menelik had entered the crater with his slaves and his treasure to 'sleep forever'. An offspring of his family, the legend says, will one day arise and restore the old glory of Ethiopia, conquering all of the land south to the Rufji River (in present day Tanzania). He will ascend Kilimanjaro and recover the gold jewels of his ancestor among which will be a ring, the seal of Solomon, which Menelik was wearing. His descendant will place the ring on his own finger and will be immediately endowed with Solomon's wisdom. Which surely means that he, like most normal people who find themselves gasping for breath at the top of Africa's highest mountain, will get himself back down to Horombo Hut as fast as his legs will carry him.

From the Tropics to the Arctic

The flora and fauna of Mt. Kilimanjaro

The Great Green Silence – the Kilimanjaro Rainforest

The windward sectors of the forest

Kilimanjaro, as we have seen, is not beyond the reach of the maritime winds and weather patterns. The 'long rains', usually occurring between mid-March and mid-May, sweep in on the south-easterly monsoon. In consequence, the southerly slopes of Kilimanjaro receive almost twice as much rain as the northerly-facing flanks, which explains why the forests in the lee of the mountain are noticeably less deep and dense, and somewhat different in character, from their counterparts on the windward slopes.

It is in those forest zones that most of the water found on Kilimanjaro (an estimated and astonishing ninety-six per cent) originates. The broad circlet of trees and other vegetation, warm and damp, often encourages a corresponding girdle of cloud and, even when the seasonal rains are not lashing down upon the leafy canopy, the trees might drip with condensing mist. Water from rain or mist is soaked up by the mat of decomposing leaves on the forest floor, to be processed through the natural water filter of humus and porous volcanic rock. It runs underground along less porous strata of lava to emerge as springs lower down the slopes, where much of it is channelled into the ancient and modern irrigation systems of the Chagga.

The cultivated lower slopes of Kilimanjaro are networked by these irrigation furrows, more than a thousand of them, channelled from streams and ingeniously led round precipitous ledges, across gullies and under boulders, sometimes for distances of 17 or 18 kilometres. It is the Chagga's life-support system and a tribute to their industry and ingenuity. But there are no boundaries, tribal or international, in the mountain's prodigality – its waters also seep or flow down to the semi-arid plains to be processed, with the well-chewed grasses, through the sacred stomachs of the Maasai cows; the waters swell rivers as well as udders. To the south they roll down, brown with the silt of Africa, through rocks studded with garnet along the Pangani River to the Indian Ocean, powering the turbines of several hydroelectric plants as they pass through. To the north, they drain into Kenya's Tsavo River which enters the ocean as the Sabaki.

Kilimanjaro's aquarian role as water bearer is obviously of immense importance to the cultivators and plains dwellers who benefit from its providence. What is less obvious is the role played by the mountain's so-called 'lower' plants, a superficially uninspiring group which embraces the bryophytes (the mosses and liverworts) and the lichens. 120 species of lichen and 596 species of mosses and liverworts are known on the mountain. Lichens, apart from being good indicators of the cleanliness of the air, are among the oldest living things on Earth, and are actually two organisms in one; a combination of algae and fungus living in symbiosis. United they stand and asunder they would often fall – lichens can grow where algae or fungi could not 'go it alone', a remarkable marriage of convenience brought about by some quirk of evolutionary development. Together, the two elements seem to be working out the secret of eternal youth. Some lichens are thought to be about 4,000 years old, whereas the nearest relatives of their algae and fungi components live only for a few years or even months.

Kilimanjaro's lichens remain (in that classic botanical understatement) 'imperfectly known'. But the liverworts and mosses are among the best investigated in tropical Africa, the first collection being made by von Höhnel during his unsuccessful attempt on Kibo with Count Teleki in 1887. This bryoflora is rich in endemic and rare species and thrives in a variety of habitats. Liverworts and mosses might be found on the trunks and branches of trees, the thickness of cover often exceeding, in the rainforest, the diameter of the host's trunk or branch. Or they might be found on fallen logs or

Opposite: Semi-tropical rainforest which stretches from 6,000 to 9,000 feet on the lower slopes of Mt. Kilimanjaro. Lianas, lichens and mosses festoon the camphor, cedar, juniper, olive and pillar trees flourishing in the warm humidity.

Previous pages: Smoke from cooking fires drifting through the trees at the first camp on the Machame route.

in the dripping crevices of rocky cliffs, or carpeting the forest floor among the stands of giant heather. They grow beneath the giant groundsels, in lava caves, in the inhospitable alpine desert of the Saddle and as high as 5000 metres on the western breach of Kibo. Their most unlikely hosts, in the ericaceous bush and alpine tussock belts, are decomposing leopard droppings, which at these altitudes normally consist of the hairs and bones of mice or hyrax. The droppings lie around for several years before being colonised by the moss *Tetraplodon bryoides*, which is also found in the Arctic. Liverworts and mosses might be the 'plain Janes' of the plant world, but like many plain Janes there is more to them than meets the eye.

Their contribution to water conservation is enormous. Mosses can intercept four or five times as much water from rain or mist as foliage, and it has been estimated that on Kilimanjaro, where the highest density of bryophytes coincides with the wetter southerly slopes of the rainforest (an area of approximately 200 square kilometres) the interception capacity is roughly one billion litres of water during a single rain storm. As this area is directly above the most important agricultural lands on the mountain, its importance as a water source is obvious. The water held by the lichens and mosses is released slowly and the bryophyte cover reduces evaporation, especially from the surface of the soil. This preserves soil moisture and provides a continuous supply of water to the streams, irrigation channels and the rivers that run down to the sea.

Kilimanjaro's waters might wander, but its flora and fauna are, on the whole, prisoners of their environment. In terms of species and within the boundaries of the National Park which does not, of course include the cultivated areas, approximately sixty-nine per cent of the flowering plants, seventy-eight per cent of the birds and eighty per cent of the larger mammals are to be found in the montane forest. But many species, including exotics, flourish below the forest belt in and around the Chagga fields and *shambas* and plantations. There, where climate and fertility are ideal for many plants and creatures, including man, a variety of habitats attract varieties of living things.

Many of these worlds in miniature are of course man-made or man-induced and, among the indigenous trees, shrubs and grasses, are a host of introduced species, from wheat on the south-west slopes (where the localised wind and weather systems mentioned earlier produce the right amount of rain) to arabica coffee on the plantations and bananas and maize in the *shambas*. Less useful but more beautiful plants may be found growing wild, including pink or purple clovers, a blue-flowered pea, a pink *Clematis* and a relative of the African Violet.

Above this settled and cultivated zone lies the true and natural forest. Strictly speaking it should not, perhaps, be known as rainforest, if this is deemed to be forest which enjoys at least ten months a year without a water deficit. But the name is commonly employed and for the purpose of this book seems justified for the tree belt on Kilimanjaro, so little known, certainly has much in common with rainforests elsewhere. Away from the few tracks it encloses the intruder in an apparently timeless and secretive silence broken only by the occasional call of birds or monkeys, or the wind whispering through the canopy, or the drip of raindrops. Sun as well as rain is filtered down through the foliage, its rays minted into coins of light and flung generously across the forest floor.

The predominating silence, like the tranquility of the African bush, is deceptive. Everything in the forest is fighting for its life in an endless, primeval war, no less violent because the screams are silent and the blood is green. It is a war

Right: Forest moss, common throughout the rainforest.

Below: St. John's wort, usually found in temperate regions, but also growing at high altitude in the tropics.

99

Above: *Soft lighting illuminates the delicate formation of a young fern leaf.*

Top: *Impatiens Kilimanjari, a kind of 'Busy Lizzy', is unique to Kilimanjaro's rainforest.*

Left: *A small mountain stream running through the dense forest.*

waged largely with chemical weapons for almost every plant, from the tallest tree to the slightest blade of grass, is obliged to create food from carbon dioxide, chlorophyll and light, or die. Photosynthesis, that magical 'force that through the green fuse drives the flower' drives the green age of the forest. Man has created nothing to match it and his life, as much as that of a single blade of grass, depends upon it.

Battles rage below and above the ground. Roots thrust and probe for mineral-enriched water, branches reach and claw for light and air, and the weak go to the wall. Or rather to the earth from which they struggled in vain. Everywhere, among the virility of vibrant green shoots and saplings, among the sturdy tree trunks and muscular vines, among the bright flowers and aromatic herbs, there is the putrifying clutter of death and decay. The rainforest is its own battlefield and graveyard with its own living monuments, and wreaths, and flowers, in honour of the dead.

And the rainforest's dead are worthy of honour for, without them, there would eventually be no life. There is a satisfying appropriateness in the fact that the earth's rainforests are mostly found in the so-called Third World where so little goes to waste. In a country where old tyres are made into shoes, where empty boxes and bottles are prized, it is fitting that the forest sets such a fine example in the science of recycling. Africa is untidy. Its natural litter lies everywhere, hampering fastidious visitors by blocking forest tracks, or puncturing inner tubes in the bush, or offending civilised eyes and nostrils with the sights and stench of violent death. But Africa's forests, like Africa's poor, are never wasteful. Every leaf which spirals down, every stem which wilts, every flower which fades, pays its death duties to the earth. In minerals, the coin of the realm.

So life goes on. And among its forms are some fascinating species. Wild dates and ferns choke the sunless river gorges of the southern slopes, where the occasional wild fig clings with claw-like roots to the steep sides or thrusts down through the chaos of boulders to the water table. On the forested ridges between the gorges grows a variety of trees which prefer the wetter conditions found on this sector of the mountain. Among them is the Lemonwood *Xymalos monospora* its bark conspicuously disfigured by rectangles and whorls and its leaves distinctively quilted. Its common name derives from the lemon-yellow colour of its heartwood. Other trees include a species of wild poplar with heart-shaped leaves, (*Macaranga kilimandscharica*), and the subdominant but plentiful (*Agauria salicifolia*), a gnarled tree with a rough reddish bark and, when in blossom, spikes of pink, heather-like flowers.

Two large and economically important trees which thrive in this wetter habitat are the East African Camphorwood, (*Ocotea usambarensis*), which can achieve a height of forty metres and a girth, in exceptional cases, of eight metres, and (*Podocarpus milanjianus*), perhaps the most characteristic tree of East Africa's montane forests. Both trees occur throughout the southern forest between about two-and-a-half to three thousand metres and yield fine timber. Camphorwood is one of the best utility hardwoods, its timber giving off the strong, aromatic scent implicit in the name. The Podo produces straight-grained timber of a fine and even texture, uniform and pale yellow in colour, giving the tree its common name 'Yellowwood'. It is a heavily exploited softwood in East Africa, and a relative of the pines. Like pines (which are not native to East Africa) Podo is an evergreen, littering the forest floor with its slender but robust leaves and its small green berries.

The berries, together with the fruits and leaves of certain other trees and shrubs, are eaten and dispersed by the monkeys, turacos and hornbills which inhabit the forest. The monkeys – there are two species in the rainforest – are named after their colours, the Blue monkey and the Black-and-White colobus, and both are quite beautiful. The Blue monkey has a fairly widespread distribution throughout central, eastern and south-eastern Africa, and is nowhere as colourful as its name suggests, but the sub-species found on Kilimanjaro, *Cercopthecus mitis kibonotensis*, has a bluish tinge to the dark greys of its lovely thick fur. It is not uncommon in the lower parts of the forest and is strictly diurnal, moving around in small groups. Blue monkeys are relatively large and sturdy, but quieter on the move than smaller species. Territorial rights are proclaimed by a repeated, loud 'Peoo!' especially at sunrise and sunset, confusing the uninitiated bird enthusiast.

The Black-and-White colobus is another large monkey, more slender than the Blue and even more beautiful, the Kilimanjaro sub-species, *Colobus guereza caudata*, being strikingly so. All eastern colobus are black with white facial surrounds and streaming snow-white capes, but the tails of the Kilimanjaro colobus are more bushy and almost completely white. To see a family or colony of these monkeys leaping or catapulting through the tall forest trees, the shafts of sunlight catching, for a moment, the streaming white fur of cape and tail, is a memorable experience.

Their acrobatic adroitness is achieved without the help of thumbs for colobus, unlike all other monkeys, don't posses them. Like the Blue monkeys they are diurnal, but they feed mainly on leaves rather than fruit and consequently have less need to descend from their high-rise home in the canopy. Their territorial call is a collectively guttural and purring roar which, when made by a whole colony, rings through the forest with a belling, haunting resonance.

In a habitat of limited visibility communication by sound is obviously important to the creatures which want to make their presence known. One of the most characteristic sounds of the Kilimanjaro rainforest is the loud croaking call of the only turaco found on the mountain, Hartlaub's (*Tauraco hartlaubi*), endemic to East Africa. This pigeon-sized bird which feeds on fruits and berries, is mainly dark green shading into violet blue above and apple green below, perfect camouflage among the sheaves of foliage. But when it flap-glides across a forest glade its most prominent feature is the crimson flash of its flight feathers. Even in the gloom of the forest the crimson is eye-catching, the colour deriving from pigmentation rather than the optical illusion caused by refraction of light, as is the case with many other birds.

The only hornbill on Kilimanjaro, the Silvery-cheeked (*Bycanistes brevis*), makes up for its singularity by size and noise. It is big and powerful enough to create a clearly audible 'whoosh' as it thrashes its way to feed and to roost, and its raucous braying and grunting sends small shock-waves of sound across the upper valleys of Chaggaland or through the forest. Despite its size and its huge bill it regularly feeds on figs and smaller fruits, though it is also – sometimes aggressively – carnivorous, taking birds' eggs, nestlings, termites, centipedes and even fruit bats. Red-fronted parrots (Poicephalus) and Green pigeons (*Treron australis*), like the hornbills, are drawn to fruiting trees. The parrots are fond of the berries of the podocarpus, and even their flowers; the pigeons love wild figs. These apple-green doves are difficult to see when feeding, their plumage blending so well with the foliage of the figs. But when focused through the lenses of binoculars they turn out to be anything but dull, the warm green of their bodies set off by the coral red cere on the bill and their coral red legs.

The forest has many interesting and beautiful birds, among them the uncommon Green ibis (*Bostrychia olivacea*) and Black duck (*Anas sparsa*), the massive, monkey-eating Crowned eagle (*Stephanoaetus coronatus*) and the relatively tiny White-starred bush robin (*Pogonocichla stellata*), a delightful, robin-like bird, yellow below with a slate-blue head and

Above: *A thoughtful expression on the face of a Black and White Colobus monkey.*

Left: *Vulturine Guinea-fowl.*

Bottom: *The Bushbuck, a shy denizen of the forests.*

Below: *Yellow-necked spurfowl.*

Above: The curious but watchful gaze of a leopard in the forest.

olive green mantle. It has a small white spot in front of each eye and a black-bordered white spot on the lower throat.

Birding in the rainforest can be frustrating and hard on the neck. The secret is to start at dawn, if not before, and to find a fruiting tree or hope to encounter that forest phenomenon, a 'bird-wave'. Such 'waves' are often inspired by safari ants, which whisper through the forest in a dark, determined and deadly procession, devouring such creatures, dead or alive, which they encounter and which cannot escape. Few birds actually feed on ants but the birds of the forest have learned to use the columns of safari ants (*siafu* in Kiswahili) as 'beaters', flushing out insects or other small creatures which they – the birds – gratefully intercept. Life at the wrong end of the food chain is uncluttered by choice, and very, very finite.

A bird party on Kilimanjaro might include Fischer's (*Phyllastrephus debilis*) or mountain greenbuls (*P. placidus*), the Olive thrush, (*Turdus abyssinicus*) Ruppell's robin chat (*Cossypha semirufa*) and the Brown Woodland warbler (*Phylloscopus umbrovirens*). High above such brief flurries of activity, in the canopy, Kenrick's starlings, or even that other starling of the highland forest, the uncommon and highly localised Abbott's might be seen by those birders with limitless patience, strong neck muscles and good binoculars. Forest glades are easier hunting grounds and might yield the Black roughwing swallow, the Scaly francolin or, near the lower edges of the forest belt, the attractive representative of that most attractive genus, the Cinnamon-Chested bee-eater, larger but similar in colour to its lowland equivalent, the Little bee-eater. Bee-eaters, needless to say, live mostly on honey-bees (though they will take other winged insects) devenoming the bee by rubbing it against a convenient branch to remove the sting.

Other animals and birds inhabit the forest but are not easily seen, partly because of the screens of vegetation, partly because forest birds and animals tend to be shy, but mostly because few people venture from the limited number of established tracks. Even if they did they would be lucky (though they might not think so at the time!) to encounter that shy but most adaptable of big cats, the leopard, which is perfectly at home in all areas of the forest and secure at the top of the food chain. Its prey must include monkeys, baboons, duikers, suni antelopes, bushbucks, bushbabies and bush pigs, all of which occur in the rainforest though not necessarily at all levels or in all areas.

Going down the scale in terms of size and noise, though not in number, we come to those inheritors of the earth, the insects. They are present in their usual countless abundance, though most walkers and climbers will scarcely notice them, apart from the butterflies. The larger and more spectacular of these are the swallowtails among which are the Regal (*Papilio rex*) Horniman's (*Papilio hornimani*) and the Kilimanjaro swallowtail (*Papilio sjostedti*). Horniman's swallowtail is as beautiful as most of its genus but like other butterflies and many beauties it has its unlovely habits, in this case a prediliction for soil dampened by elephant urine. The Kilimanjaro swallowtail is known only from Kilimanjaro and nearby Mount Meru and Ngorongoro, though the subspecies atavus is restricted to Kilimanjaro.

The flowers on which many of the butterflies feed are not as prolific, in numbers or species, as many visitors might expect. The rainforest is festooned with foliate lichens or the grey-green wire-wool of Old Man's Beard, not drooping with large showy orchids or sprung with floral swathes, daubing the forest floor in the primary colours of the tropics. It is not a giant natural greenhouse, all 'grow-bags' and computer-controlled micro-climates and tender loving care. Its plants are fighting their environment as well as each other and, in this endless battle for survival and supremacy, being big or bright or plentiful isn't always an advantage.

Most of the flowers of the forest are small and unpretentious with a deceptively delicate beauty. One of the loveliest is *Begonia meyeri-johannis*, its white petals tinged with pink and set off by the central clump of golden anthers. Along the forest tracks there are clovers (*Trifolium spp.*) a genus which need phosphorus and find it in the volcanic soils. There are small blue pea flowers (*Parochetus communis*) and yellow sunflecks (*Guizotia reptans*), and many species of balsam, a family found in all tropical and sub-tropical regions. Most of the balsams belong to the genus *Impatiens* of which the best known are the 'Busy Lizzies; The best known balsam on Kilimanjaro is *Impatiens kilimanjari*, which is found nowhere else in the world. The flowers of many *impatiens* are sometimes mistaken, for orchids by the casual observer. Most of them are pink, but there are white ones with purple specks and a variety which is bright red. The Kilimanjaro endemic has a flower befitting its global rarity (it is fairly common on the mountain itself). It is small but striking especially when illuminated by the sharp mountain light, when its red flower glows above the yellow inward curving spur of the lower sepal.

Walkers and climbers on the Marangu Route will find this exciting endemic flower quite easily if they look. They might even see the Horniman's swallowtail which sips elephant urine from the freshly soaked earth. But they won't see dark patches of elephant urine on the track, or elephant droppings, or elephants, for most of the larger game on Kilimanjaro is now to be found in the western and northern tracks of forest. Elephants, which numbered well over a thousand a few decades ago and many more than that at the turn of the century, have been reduced by poaching and loss of habitat to about two hundred and twenty, though the figures vary due to seasonal movements between the mountain and the nearby Kenyan sanctuaries of Amboseli and Tsavo West. On Kilimanjaro elephants are now generally distributed between the Namwai and Tarakia Rivers, along the lower northern slopes.

Rhino are perhaps extinct on the mountain though a few still survive in Amboseli. Buffalo populations have also suffered, though being mainly grazers they have always been restricted, in the forest zone, to areas where glades are large or plentiful. Giraffe are sometimes seen in the forest and other larger mammals, such as lions, occasionally pass through on their way to more open country above or below the belt of trees.

Above: *A herd of elephants crosses a dry pan in Amboseli National Park.*

The leeward sectors of the rainforests

The animals found in these western and northern tracts of forest would, on the whole, be just as comfortable, if not more so, on the wetter southern and eastern slopes if they were not disturbed. The same is not true of the vegetation. There, in the rain-shadow of the mountain, certain plants thrive in the drier climate while others, common on the southerly slopes, grow less vigorously or not at all. The dominant tree of the western and northern forests is the evergreen African Pencil Cedar, *Juniperus procera*, which grows to a height of 40 metres or more. It has a fluted, sharply tapering bole and is related to the common European juniper, the berries of which were once used to flavour gin. The Pencil cedar is used commercially for furniture and joinery and, of course, in the manufacture of pencils. Cedarwood oil, used in soaps and perfumes, is distilled from its sawdust.

Another evergreen growing in the drier high altitude mist forests is the African Holly, *Ilex mitis*. Like its European cousin it bears crimson berries, much sought after by birds, but it lacks the familiar spiky leaves which decorate so many western homes – and a good many Christmas cards and puddings – each December. Its properties, from a commercial point of view, are inferior to the European Holly and its timber has little value.

There are chestnuts, too, on Kilimanjaro, but you will not find their fruits roasting over braziers on the icy pavements of London's Oxford Street, for these are the Cape chestnuts, *Calodendrum capensis*, whose striking pink blossoms make up for, in beauty, what the fruits lack in epicurean appeal. The epicures would also be disappointed by the fruits of the African Olive, two species of which are common in these drier regions of the forest. The wild olives are edible, but bitter to refined human tastes. And the 'Bastard Onionwood', as *Cassipourea malosana* is called in South Africa, has little connection with onions, though it is very common in the area and in similar montane forest throughout northern Tanzania. One small tree of these regions which might excite the sense of smell if not the taste buds is the Curry Bush (*Hypericum lanceolatum*). Its small narrow leaves give off a distinct smell of curry, though they are not the leaves used, by some East African Asians, to flavour curries and the spicy 'bitings' or snack foods known as *chevra*. The genus Hypericum was dedicated by the monks of the Middle Ages to St. John the Baptist, and most of its species are commonly known as 'St. John's wort', the old word 'wort' meaning 'a plant having medicinal properties'.

Species of podocarpus grow here and so does the Brittlewood (*Nuxia congesta*), which after the rains enlivens the shades of forest green with clusters of white flowers. The podo are evergreen and cone-bearing but their resemblance to their relatives the pines can be misleading. True pines are not indigenous to East Africa but the Patula pine (*Pinus patula*) has been introduced as a fast-growing timber tree and, together with a species of cypress (*Cupressus lusitanica*), forms the primary softwood plantation species on Kilimanjaro. Two plantations have been established, one at Rongai in the north-east and the other at West Kilimanjaro. The softwoods planted in the west not only replaced indigenous forest but also a number of large glades, deliberately kept open through the use of fire, by Maasai herders. Both plantations now extend almost to the heathland, thus breaking the natural continuity of the rainforest and effectively isolating the northern sector from the southern.

And so Kilimanjaro's rainforest, like rainforests everywhere, is in retreat, its wonderful diversity of plants and animals threatened in some cases to the point of imminent local extinction. Measures to counter this degradation are being planned and acted upon, and are discussed in a later chapter. Meanwhile, most of the forest is intact, and the experience

Opposite: First campsite on the Umbwe route on the southern flanks of the mountain.

of wandering even a little way through its green silences has as much to do with the soul as with the body. While the Kilimanjaro forest is relatively young it has the power, common to all extensive rainforests, to reduce the human intruder to respectful silence, almost awe. Below the high-vaulted roof of its canopy, among the natural, haphazard columns of its countless naves, and choirs screened with tree-fern and liana and moss-grown ruins of once mighty trees, this wild, unkempt cathedral exerts its ancient, unspoken, effortless authority upon the human mind and soul. Man and the lifetime of man and the achievements of man are reduced, if only for a while, to insignificance. And yet the experience uplifts and enhances. There, in the clear fragmented light which throws the stained-glass greens and yellows across and between the shadowy columns, is a rare tranquillity, a peace of mind, a benediction bestowed upon the present by the ageless past.

Above: Old Man's Beard graces the lower branches of a forest tree.

Most of the flowers of the forest are small and unpretentious with a deceptively delicate beauty.

The High Moors

Kilimanjaro is unique in many ways, one of which, among the higher volcanic mountains of East Africa, is the lack of a bamboo zone which usually occurs between the altitudes of 2 - 3000 metres. Bamboo grows on Mount Meru, just a little to the west of Kilimanjaro, but not on the great White Mountain itself. No one really knows why – there are a lot of things that no one really knows about Kilimanjaro – though a slightly drier climate has been put forward as an explanation.

Near the upper limit of Kilimanjaro's true forest where stands of bamboo would normally be found, the forest begins to change in composition. Podo, African holly, camphorwood, African rosewood (*Hagenia abyssinica*) and the giant St John's wort (*Hypericum revolutum*), are conspicuous at these altitudes together with dense but spindly thickets of *Philippia excelasa*, one of the giant heaths. Another 'tree heather', *Erica arborea*, related to the famous 'lucky white heather' of Scotland but with trunks six metres high and half-a-metre thick, forms an enchanted forest, bearded with lichen, a little further down the wetter slopes.

The African rosewood has big compound leaves, its attractive, drooping blossoms made up of clusters of dark reddish flowers, while the flowers of the St John's wort are golden yellow, each unfolding in solitary splendour at the end of branches neatly spiked with lanceolate leaves of polished green. And another plant with golden yellow flowers is found here, one of Kilimanjaro's three endemic giant groundsels, *Senecio Johnstonii*. This particular groundsel is by no means common, though in its favoured habitat, the seepage zones on the mountain's wetter slopes, it tends to occur in small, dominant clumps. It belongs to the same genus as the common groundsel (*Senecio vulgaris*) which in Europe is often fed to cage birds, but the budgerigars would have problems with the giants of Kilimanjaro and a rather large cage would be needed. *Senecio johnstonii* sometimes attains a height of nine metres, the branchlets of its high, open structured crowns topped with the large panicles of its flower head.

The trees of these upper edges of the rainforest are clad with mosses, lichens and epiphytic ferns. Numerous other ferns fledge the glades of this timberline region and among and between the trees and heaths, enjoying more space and light as the rainforest reaches its limits with generally smaller and more scattered trees, is a comparatively rich undergrowth. A variety of shrubs, with red or porcelain blue berries, with blossoms of white or mauve or pale yellow, find life acceptable, if not easy, at the upper edge of the forest. And wildflowers grow in relative abundance. Climbers, including the lovely, sweet-scented *Begonia meyeri-johannis*, showy-flowered *Acanthaceae*, pink balsams, red-hot pokers and cool little violets decorate the glades and shady recesses of the forest's final fling.

Above the timberline on the southerly side of the mountain is a zone of subalpine ericacious heath, dominated by *Philippia*, with the tiny leaves and bell-like white flowers so typical of the heathers. On the drier northern side this zone extends into one of ericacious bush where other heaths or heath-like species hold sway. Significant examples are *Anthospermum usambarensis*, reminiscent of cypress, and *Stoebe kilimandscharica*, its branchlets like slender, silvery grey plaits.

The heathland is superficially drab, its predominant shades subdued and the form of its larger plants unstriking. But the eyes and mind of an Emily Bronte would have seen in the heaths and gorse-like shrubs and the multitude of grasses, in the flocculent ridges and slopes which lean and roll and climb into the upland grasslands, a wild but quiet beauty, powerful enough to liberate the restless soul. It is indeed, after the seductive but possessive beauty of the rainforest, a

Opposite: A Giant Groundsel in the foreground of this unusual view of Kilimanjaro.

place of enlightenment for the African skies, screened for so long by the black lace shawl of the silhouetted canopy, are suddenly set free.

The light strikes down on another plethora of plants, but out in these open spaces individual species are often easier to examine and admire. Among the grasses may be found one of the finest of the East African gladioli, *(watsonioides)*, its lovely drooping flowers red or salmon pink. Th re is a pink-flowered iris (*Dierama pendulum*), a white anemone (*thomsonii*), a blue and a white clover (*Trifolium cryptopodium* and *burchellianum*) and an orchid with a spike of pink flowers (*Disa stairsit*). One of the lobelias (*holstii*) grows there too, and so does the familiar red-hot poker (*Kniphofia thomsonii*) which, like the anemone, was named for that mildly eccentric Scot who crossed Maasailand.

There is also a remarkable group of daisies, the flowers of the 'golden spiral' genus, *Helichrysun*. These stiff, dry and prickly-looking blooms have achieved both fame and immortality. They are the flowers from which porters once made garlands to be placed around the necks of those who had conquered the White Mountain. And they are *les immortelles*, the 'everlasting flowers'. The actual flowers, immortal or otherwise, are inconspicuous. It is the enveloping, petal-like bracts that are coloured red with a pink centre, as in *Helichrysum meyer-johannis*, or greenish-white (*H. argyranthum*) yellow (*H. cymosum*) or yellow-brown (*H. kilimanjari*), which also has lemon scented leaves.

The interesting variations of form and substance in the plants of Kilimanjaro's upper regions are largely responses to the increasingly severe conditions imposed by altitude. Just beyond the edges of the timberline, nights may already, at 3,000 metres, be frosty, while daytime temperatures could rise to 15 C. The stiff dry structure of the everlasting flowers helps them to survive in the constant struggle against the elements while other plants, especially out on the upland grasslands, have developed other strategies. One successful and beautiful structure for survival is the rosette, a convoluted system of overlapping leaves or bracts which can open and close to regulate light, temperature or moisture levels.

The best examples of this natural engineering are to be found higher up the mountain but the flowers of one, the protea, grace the heath as well as the upland grasslands. The family is composed of evergreen trees, shrubs or plants, most of which are found in southern Africa and Australia. In fact the emblem of South Africa is a protea. On Kilimanjaro the most common species is, appropriately, *Protea kilimandscharica*, the 'sugar bush' which grows up to four-and-a-half-metres tall. When fully open the flowers themselves are about five centimetres across, a mass of upright white filaments springing from a rosette of bracts in the form of a shallow bowl.

If the everlasting flowers and the protea need help with high altitude engineering, the grasses, those storm troopers of the barren wilderness, need all the back-up they can muster. They move in where whole regiments of plants fear to spread. Like all shock troops they need a secure base from which to operate, a reliable supply line – as invulnerable to attack as possible – the ability to capitalise quickly upon their gains and as much support or relief as they can get. And they need the right equipment for the conditions. The high altitude grasses specialise in such operations. They rely on extensive root systems, safe from frost and fire (the heathland is particularly prone to damage by fire). They mature quickly, while the going is good and they consolidate and replace their numbers by a high reproduction rate. And their leaves are thin and tough and often formed into dense squads or tufts, all of which helps them survive the onslaught of hostile natural forces.

Above: *Everlasting flowers, common in the high altitude areas of the mountain.*

Above (left): *The delicate blossoms of a Mountain Thistle.*

Left: *Red and yellow versions of the Red hot poker growing wild on the moorland.*

117

Above: *A close-up of the head of a Giant Lobelia.*

In the field and in the mass, soldiers are a neutral coloured, unappealing horde. Individually they can sometimes be handsome and interesting. So it is with the Kilimanjaro grasses, fighting for a foothold and survival on the high heath and moor. Tussock grasses, blue-stem grasses, fescue, unicorn grass and crested hair grass are some of the mountain grasses to be seen in the upland heath and meadows – or more often to be overlooked. Grasses form the largest family of living plants and one water-grass alone – we call it rice – feeds more than half the world. One half of Africa is covered by grass yet few people, other than farmers and botanists, take an interest in these quite amazing plants. This indifference is a pity because the slender forms and delicately intricate flower heads of many grasses are as beautiful, in their own unassuming way, as other more spectacular flowers and blossoms. And the grasses of Kilimanjaro are no exception.

The transformation from ericaceous heath to moorland is difficult to define as certain plants or groups of plants persist throughout both altitude levels, one example being *Erica arborea*, the giant heather. But the ongoing struggle against the elements and the altitude begins to cut most plants, as it begins to cut most men, down to size. There on the exposed slopes of the high moors the tree heathers are reduced to the height of a man, one sixth of their size at the upper levels of the rainforest. But the true indicators of altitude contradict this general rule for the plants which catch the eye of the most casual observer, and announce that they are going up in the world, belong to another race of giants.

Lobelia deckenii is the only giant lobelia found on the mountain. Botanists consider it a very close relative of the small lobelia familiar, as a bedding plant, to so many gardeners. Yet the monsters of Kilimanjaro can grow half as high as a giraffe. In form they resemble the symbolic phallus, or *lingam*, which represents the God Siva in certain Hindu temples. But these natural phallic symbols are far more complex and beautiful than their stone counterparts in India. The hollow stemmed flower stalk springs from a tufted rosette of slender leaves which protect the non-flowering rosette buds by enclosing them at night in a life-saving embrace. At the same time the leaf rosettes exude a watery fluid, a natural anti-freeze, which gives the plant extra protection and its nickname, the gin-and-tonic lobelia.

The flower stalk itself is a geometrically elegant arrangement of tongue-like bracts which conceal the blue flowers within. These pretty flowers are sought by sunbirds, the Scarlet-tufted Malachite (*Nectarinia johnstoni*) and the Tacazze (*Nectarinia tacazze*), which in fact are not seeking nectar but the tiny Bibonid flies which live and breed in the bases of the lobelia flowers. During their feeding flurries the sunbirds often shred the bracts of the flower stalks with their restless little feet.

These particular sunbirds are relatively large members of a most attractive and colourful family, the 'humming birds of Africa' on a larger scale, though sunbirds and humming birds are not related. The male Scarlet-tufted Malachite is a brilliant metallic green when seen in clear light, with bright red pectoral tufts and long central tail feathers. Despite its busy wings it is, like so many living things, a prisoner of circumstance. It is rarely, if ever, found below 3,000 metres or above 4,500.

The Tacazze, named after a river in northern Ethiopia, is even more beautiful but it too is confined to a narrow habitat in terms of altitude, ranging from 1,800 to 4,200 metres. The male Tacazze, like its lobelia-loving counterpart, has long central tail feathers and, at about 23 centimetres long, is almost as big. In poor light it appears black but when struck by sunbeams it is transformed into a scintillating iridescent violet. A much smaller sunbird, the Eastern Double-collared (*Cinnyris mediocris*), is also found on the heath and on the fringes of the moorland but the Olive sunbird (*Cyanomitra olivacea*), reaches its altitude limits in the lower parts of the rainforest.

The sunbirds which frequent the lobelias also visit other, even more fascinating outsize plants, the two endemic Giant Senecios (*kilimanjari* and *cottonii*) which grow on the Kilimanjaro moorland. *S. kilimanjari* grows into a small tree up to five metres high, bearing a large crown of leaves, a long spike of lemon-yellow flowers. *S. cottonii* is found (it cannot be missed when it is around) in the same area, but extends further up the mountain to about 4,000 metres, populating the alpine bogs and seepage zones beneath Mawenzi with unearthly dynasties of dark, forboding forms.

To be alone in the silence of a grove of *Senecio cottonii*, their shaggy elephantine stalks and limbs topped with great rosettes of leaves and half-obscured with cold and swirling mists, is an almost disturbing experience, as if you had been awakened from a restless sleep to find yourself on some lost world, surrounded by mummified monsters. It isn't so much the grotesque appearance of the plants in itself that unsettles the imaginative mind, or a sense of wonder at the workings of evolution, but the overwhelming feeling that they should not exist at all: that plants like these should have died out with the dinosaurs. There is nothing else on earth quite like them, and they are found only on East African mountains.

Unusual conditions produce unusual life-forms, and conditions at the edge of the tropical alpine zones are unusual enough. The trees senecios, twice as tall as a man, are highly specialized answers to highly specific demands. They, like the lobelias, have a thirst to match their giant proportions which explains why they grow in the upland swamps. But water freezes at night at these altitudes so the supply must be insulated, just as water pipes in temperate climes are sometimes lagged against the extreme cold of winter.

The Giant Senecio is lagged with leaves. The plant grows slowly, perhaps taking a hundred years to achieve maturity. As it grows, the leaves of the rosette which protect its life-force, the vulnerable growing shoot, die off but do not fall. Instead they enclose the massive stalk with a sheath of dry leaves. A further adaptation allows water flow to continue even in the early hours of the day when the huge plant badly needs to get on with its mammoth drinking bout when the ground is still frozen and impedes flow from the roots. The plant has a hard layer of thin-walled, open cells just beneath the insulating sheath of leaves which acts as a reservoir system when the normal flow is restricted. This layer of cells, like the cellular aluminium shell of an aircraft, also gives the Senecio strength and lightness which is why its clumsy, top-heavy structure doesn't easily collapse in the testing bleakness of these Afro-alpine moors.

There are two smaller Senecios in the moorland regions, one, *S. meyeri-johannis*, being a mat-like herb and the other, *S. purtschelleri*, more shrubby and like all the groundsels they have heads of yellow flowers. Other flowers, many of them of the 'everlasting' varieties, flourish among yet another tribe of giants, the tussock grasses, the largest and most common of which is *Pentaschistis minor*. Despite its specific name it forms the largest tussocks which can be a metre high, their centres a dense mass of compacted dead grasses, their outer, living grasses forming a ring or crescent. In wetter places the tussock grass *Festuca pilgeri* forms dense, almost impenetrable waist-high clumps. These giant grasses, like the senecios, have 'learned' to overcome the insulation problem through a similar strategy – the protection of the living by the dead.

Insulation is a problem for animals too. Many of them solve it without too much fuss – they move and they grow thicker coats, just like the tourists. But it is still a little surprising to find animals such as eland regularly inhabiting the sub-alpine and alpine zone, almost to 5,000 metres on the Saddle. Largest of the antelope, the eland has been called 'the apotheosis

Above: Needle ice forms in the cold mornings of the Shira Plateau.

Left: Frost on the flowers and ferns on the Shira Plateau.

Right: Eland are still seen on the saddle between the peaks of Kibo and mawenzi.

Below: Lions still very occasionally penetrate the forest in search of prey.

of antelope evolution'. Its ox-like appearance, down on the plains and in open bush where it is most often encountered, occasionally singles it out as acceptable 'meat-on-the-hoof' for the Maasai who traditionally don't eat game. But appearances deceive. The eland has a specialized diet, is adapted to ranging widely to satisfy it and can withstand dry conditions, going without water for a week or perhaps a month if necessary. And despite its bulk (it weighs about 900 kilogrammes, as much as a small adult rhino) it can leap two metres into the air with apparent ease.

Walkers and climbers will be fortunate to see eland and more fortunate still to get close to them, for they are shy animals which normally start to trot away, head high, long before a photographer or hunter can get within reasonable range. The Grey duiker is also fairly common in the heathland. Red duikers and bushbuck are sometimes seen above the tree line, and, more occasionally, buffalo. Elephant have been known, from time to time, to traverse the Shira, reaching an altitude, like the eland, of close to 5000 metres, but these days tend to keep as low a profile as elephants can manage.

Lions very occasionally penetrate the forest and wander across the Shira, and a pack of five wild dogs was encountered, in 1962, above the snowline of Kibo. The dogs followed a party of walkers to the summit but made no attempt to attack the party. In 1979 a porter called David was not so lucky. He was, it seems, set upon by a small pack of dogs as he walked alone across the moorland above Mandara Hut. It must have been a frightening experience – wild dogs, the 'painted wolves' of Africa, kill their prey by tearing it apart, usually beginning at the groin. Fortunately for the porter a party of tourists arrived, causing the dogs to retreat but not before David had lost the little finger of his right hand.

Another large carnivore has been to the top of Kibo, as Ernest Hemingway recorded in *The Snows of Kilimanjaro*. The famous frozen leopard discovered on the rim of the crater in the 1920s was seen by various people and photographed but its carcase, preserved by the freezer-like conditions, disappeared, its epitaph being only the name of the place where it once lay. 'What was it doing there?' is the much asked question. Probably just being a leopard, wanting to see what it could find around the next bend, or in this case above the next ridge. Curiosity, it seems, killed the cat.

Leopards, however, are not uncommon on the mountain and their droppings, fibrous with the hairs of small rodents such as four-striped mice and mole rats, might be found throughout the moorland and the alpine zone, as high as the base of Kibo or Mawenzi. Melanistic leopards, the legendary 'black panthers', are sometimes recorded. They are, of course, just darker versions of the common leopard, *Panthera pardus*. When aroused to anger the leopard is single-minded in its ferocity, but when left alone they are harmless – at least to humans. It is highly unlikely that walkers will encounter leopards in any area of the mountain, and if they do the chances are that they will only get a fleeting glimpse of the charismatic 'cat who walks alone'.

Two other attractive carnivores live on and around the heath and moorland, the serval, another spotted cat, and the civet, which is also spotted and sometimes referred to as a cat, although it belongs to the same family (*Viverridae*) as the genet and the mongoose. The serval is leggy and large-eared with a short tail, the dark spots on its tawny coat solid, like those of the cheetah, rather than the rosettes of the leopard. It is somewhere between a domestic cat and a leopard in size.

The civet is also relatively long in the legs but shorter at the shoulder, standing about 40 cm high. Its pale greyish coat is heavily spotted and blotched with black, and its long, dog-like face is masked in black across the eyes. For centuries the anal scent-glands of the civet have, involuntarily and ironically, worked to make women more alluring and men more foolish. The oily secretion from the glands was, and to a much lesser extent still is, used as a basis for perfumes. Perhaps for this reason, civets are predominantly nocturnal, though they are quite common and widespread in Tanzania. As they are also very bad at crossing roads they are mostly seen dead, their beautiful pelts flattened against the tarmac or murram. Fortunately, there aren't too many long distance trucks on Kilimanjaro.

What there are a lot of are four-striped grass mice which is good news for the leopards, servals and civets, and also for the augur buzzards (*Buteo angur*). There are mountain buzzards (*B. tachardus*) too, but they are said to feed on chameleons. The charming little grass mice, unlike so many creatures on Kilimanjaro, are easy to see when they are around, and if they are easy for humans to see then the Augur buzzard, its eyes having perhaps eight times the resolving power of human eyes, must have little difficulty in finding the nearest four-legged fast-food restaurant when it needs one. The eyes of the leopard and the ears of the serval are also finely tuned to movement and the civet's eyesight, especially by night, is said to be outstanding. The Four-striped grass mouse might be secure as a species, but as an individual its insurance premiums must be prohibitively high.

Augur buzzards, like all diurnal birds of prey, have stereoscopic vision so that when they do stoop to conquer they judge changing distances with assurance as they prey almost entirely on rodents. Among the easiest of raptors to identify, the buzzards, typically broad-winged, have slate-grey upperparts with a chestnut-red tail. The underparts are variable in colour, sometimes dark but often entirely white, making the birds quite distinctive when perched. Their cry, wild and clangorous and carrying, is entirely in tune with the echoing tracks of the lonely upland moors. The Mountain buzzard is smaller and browner, with no rufous in the plumage and dark, heavy spots on the underside.

The moorland is not particularly rich in birds but species to be seen include Quail (*Coturnix coturnix*), the African snipe (*Cipella nigripennis*), the Alpine swift (*Apus melba*), the Stone chat (*Saxicola torquata*), Hunter's cisticola (*Cisticola hunteri*) and the Yellow-crowned canary (*Serinus flavivertex*). Like so many moorland birds they are all relatively drab, at least at a distance. At close quarters their subtle colours and markings are intricate and aesthetically pleasing.

Two other 'little brown jobs' live on the moorland and both can be easily observed. The Streaky seed-eater (*Serinus striolatus*), often seen around Horombo Hut, is as visually unexciting as it sounds though its colouration has a certain functional beauty. The small dusky brown Alpine chat (*Cercomela sordida*) is even more difficult to overlook, as it is as engagingly 'tame' and as perkily plump as the European 'redbreast'. It might well be called – however inaccurately – the 'Kilimanjaro robin' but it is a true mountain bird, its natural habitat lying between the upper edge of the forest and about four-and-a-half thousand metres.

The range of the Alpine chat reaches cut-off point, not surprisingly, where the Alpine Desert begins. From there on man and bird and beast have to learn to live with a stark wilderness almost bereft of life, a place where 'there is summer every day and winter every night'. It is there more than anywhere, in this almost barren, often beautiful land Africa's high Arctic, that the mountain becomes itself: the symbol of a country and a continent; the Mountain of Greatness, the Mountain of Light, *Oldoiny'oibor* – the White Mountain.

Overleaf: Kibo peak after heavy overnight snowfall.

Below: An Augur buzzard surveys the terrain below for any sign of prey.

Deserta Arctica

The word 'desolate' derives from the Latin verb *desolare,* which in turn is partially derived from the adverb *'solus'*, alone. It means; 1) Left alone; lonely; 2) Destitute of; lacking; 3) Destitute of inhabitants; deserted; 4) In a ruinous condition; neglected; laid waste; bare; barren; cheerless; 5) Comfortless; forlorn; disconsolate; wretched; 6) Destitute of good quality; abandoned.

Anyone who has spent much time in the Afro-alpine zone of Kilimanjaro, above 3,800 metres or so, will see, in some of these definitions, reflections of their experience. It is indeed a lonely place, much lacking in life, water and even air, desitute of permanent or semi-permanent inhabitants, laid waste by the ravages of volcanic turmoil and erosion, bare, almost barren, cheerless, comfortless and forlorn. A desolate landscape amid the awful silent calm of Kilimanjaro's high Arctic.

But 'awful' has its definitions too, and among them are 'Inspiring awe; solemnly impressive; sublimely majestic'. And there are few mountains more solemnly impressive or sublimely majestic than the highest in Africa. Kilimanjaro might look like a giant Christmas pudding when you are gazing casually at Kibo from the sunwashed security of the plains, but from 4,000 metres its scale and seriousness dispel any doubts about its magnitude or grandeur.

The vegetation cover gradually dwindles and on the slopes of the Saddle seems, to the unobservant eye, to disappear completely. What remains is a grey-brown alpine desert littered with rocks and boulders. In this uncompromising land of extremes, light and shadow, day and night and heat and cold are dramatically polarised with few intermediate tones to blur the sharp lines between one and the other. Radiation is intense and so, in the heat of the day, are the rays of the sun as they laser down with vertical or near-vertical directness through an unresisting atmosphere. Even in the day-time, and despite the unremitting sun, persistent shadow can shiver the surface of the skin with a fever-like chill. By day the temperature in direct sunlight can reach 40 C, by night the surface of the earth freezes. The thin air which allows the sun to penetrate so freely allows the heat to escape with similar ease once the sun has lost its strength, causing temperatures to rise or fall with surprising speed in morning and evening.

The phenomenom itself is not unique to the tropics, but what is unique is the climate it creates. In temperate alpine zones the nights are relatively short during the summer, when plants are growing and maturing, and the sun's rays less vertical. On the high equatorial mountains, therefore, life in the alpine zone might be even more severe than in Europe or North America. Especially if you happen to be a plant.

Most plants are anchored to the soil by roots. In normal conditions even the tiny roots of seedlings can make themselves secure. But in the Afro-alpine extremes the nightly freezing produces needle ice in the soil, these splinters of expanding moisture pushing up the surface dirt. The needle-ice thaws in the morning sun, permitting the displaced soil to fall back into place and this daily disruption of the soil, known as solifluction, uproots young seedlings, creating deserts within deserts in the bare, moist areas where solifluction operates.

In such rigorous conditions only the hardiest plants can survive. On Kilimanjaro less than 60 species of plants (other than the so-called 'lower plants') live above 4,000 metres compared with hundreds lower down the mountain. All of these plants have developed strategies for dealing with the tough conditions and some, like the everlasting flowers and tussock grasses, survive by being tough themselves. The *Helichrysum* species have strong, woody stems and at these altitudes grow closer to the ground than their exact counterparts on the moors. The tussock grasses have thin, wiry leaves to reduce

Opposite: A porter silhouetted against low lying clouds on the moorland.

129

evaporation. These grasses stabilise the soil and retain moisture, providing protection and sustenance for other, less hardy plants which follow the pioneers and settle in their 'security zone'.

Many plants of the high altitude desert bristle with fine silvery hairs which reflect solar radiation. These hairs also provide insulation by trapping a layer of air against the leaves, thus limiting the loss of water or heat. But perhaps the most ingenious natural strategy is that adopted by a type of moss. Confronted by an environment which constantly shifts, the moss has itself learned to shift. When the earth moves, the moss moves with it, rising and falling with the needles of ice. Rootless and restless, the moss forms spheres or 'sausages' or disks around nodules of soil from which it obtains nourishment. Available moisture is soaked up with sponge-like gratitude.

Water of any kind is hard to come by, but where moisture exists and shelter is available, three Senecios, *telekii*, *meyeri-johannis* and *purtschelleri*, can still be found. The white-petalled *Arabis alpina*, surprisingly delicate in these unrelenting conditions, also grows in such favourable niches. Kilimanjaro has several plant species in common with Europe and *Arabis alpina*, apart from growing on other East African mountains, is found in the Alps and in Lapland.

The reindeer of Lapland are replaced on the Kilimanjaro Saddle by eland which frequently cross the apparently barren wastes. Apart from them, roving leopards and the occasional servals or wild dogs, animal life is scarce. The thin air, strong winds and night-time cold exclude all birds from living there, and if they did there would be little for them to eat. Except for ravens and large birds of prey (and the planes which sometimes diverge from their flight paths to pass close to Kibo) the skies over Kilimanjaro are empty of all but clouds and seven they are usually absent.

The White-necked raven (*Corvus albicollis*) is a large, heavily built bird, entirely black but for a crescent of white between the nape and the upper mantle. As with most of the crow family its bill is heavy and used largely for scavenging. It is capable of circling above the summit of Kibo but is more commonly seen around Horombo Hut where it makes an easier living foraging for scraps from the tourists. Considerable numbers of them roost on mountain cliffs above the rainforest, and alot of them fly up from the countryside below the mountain.

Of the birds of prey, the most exciting possibility on Kilimanjaro is the uncommon and unusual lammergeyer, most often seen from the Shira Plateau though the observant birder might see it from many other vantage points. A true bird of the high mountains and towering cliffs, it is now classed with vultures. It has a typical vulturine bill and in common with its kind it scavenges, associating with pastoralists in Africa and visiting refuse dumps outside Indian villages. Where it exists it is sometimes regularly seen and yet in some ways it remains an enigma, and aspects of its behaviour are sometimes interpreted, by different observers, in very different ways.

The late and much-respected Salim Ali, one of the India's foremost bird lovers, insisted that the lammergeyer 'has never been known to attack live animals'. But H B Cott, the multi-talented author of *Looking at Animals*, disagrees. He mentions accounts of Lammergeyers 'knocking chamois, goats and klipspringers off cliffs and then following to feed on the mutilated corpses'. He also says that they have been known 'to pick up tortoises and drop them'.

As the only wild goats and sheep in Africa are found in the north, and the klipspringer is locally extinct on Kilimanjaro, it is tempting to ask 'What's in it for the lammergeyer?' on Kilimanjaro. Not tortoises, it seems, for they too are absent from the mountain. Lammergeyers are basically scavengers and are well-known for their habit of picking up bones and

Above: *The Lava Tower with the summit in the background.*

131

dropping them to allow them to eat the fragments (they can eat and digest pieces up to 25 cm long) and to scoop out the exposed marrow with their long tongues. They are expert 'bomb-aimers', able to drop bones onto a 10-metre -square of rock from a height of up to 150 metres with regularity. But how often would these intriguing birds find bones on the moorland or high-altitude desert? What is more probable is that the lammergeyer actually kills live prey, such as rock hyrax or four-striped mice, though there is as yet no evidence to support this. Whatever it eats or does not eat, the distinctive silhouette of the lammergeyer, with its narrow, angled wings (almost three metres in span) and its elongated diamond-shaped tail, sometimes brings a thrill of excitement to the observant birder high on Kilimanjaro.

There are much smaller winged creatures in the Afro-alpine zone, but few of them fly, and none of those for long. Most of the insects found at these altitudes have short wings, or none at all; flying is presumably a dangerous business in the strong and sometimes bitter winds that cut across the Saddle. And so most insects opt for sedentary safety among the tussock grasses or under the profusion of rocks, or even underground. Living underground, if you are an insect in the Afro-alpine desert, isn't such a bad idea. Because where there are creatures to eat, there are usually creatures to eat them, and as if the poor insects hadn't enough to put up with in the hostile world above the moors, their little lives are placed in further jeopardy once they emerge from hiding, by a host of watchful, dark-grey spiders.

The spiders eat the insects that live on and around the Saddle and the insects, presumably, eat the lichens. But there aren't many lichens. So where does the extra food come from at altitudes up to 5,000 metres, where the highest of the Kilimanjaro spiders, species still unknown, dart around among the loose shale? The answer is blowing in the wind. . . or so it would seem. The highest inhabitants of the planet Earth live at 6,500 metres, appropriately enough on Everest, their insect prey sustained by wind-blown, edible debris from below. There is no reason to suppose that communities of insects high on Kilimanjaro are not provisioned in a similar way.

The highest plants on Kilimanjaro are the tussock grasses, if we ignore the clever little everlasting flower, *Helichrysum newii*, which was recorded at 5,670 metres in Kibo's crater. The *Helichrysum* cheated a little by growing alongside a fumarole, one of the vents which, at irregular intervals, puff out little clouds of sulphur and steam. The temperature at such fumaroles can be as high as 100 °C (the boiling point of water at sea level) thus explaining the everlasting flower's surprising survival. The upper altitude limit of the tussock grasses is about 4,700 metres and, like a good many human beings encountered at these heights, the grasses seem more dead than alive.

Awful in its Silent Calm

Kibo's deceptive Christmas-pudding outline, often seen from the Saddle in partial silhouette against the sunset flare, seems to offer no threat. Mawenzi, its own volcanic symmetry blasted and worn into crags and pinnacles and spires and spectacular dyke-swarms, looks what it is, a lonely, forbidding and potentially dangerous mountain peak. Tourists on the popular Marangu Route, on attaining the Saddle, tend to turn for a few moments to gaze upon Mawenzi and perhaps to photograph it. And then move on, towards the much more user-friendly Kibo.

Those walkers or climbers who attain its summit, or at least the crater rim, will rarely wish to explore further. But those hardy and inquisitive souls who choose to descend into the crater itself will be reminded, perhaps to their mild concern, that Kibo is dormant rather than extinct. In the latter half of this century, in fact, fumarole activity has increased. The slopes of the inner crater wall are powdered by red, brown or yellow deposits of sulphur, giving off their typically unpleasant smell. It is by these fumaroles that little colonies of plants are beginning to form, taking advantage of the warmer conditions.

The inner crater itself is named after the German missionary, the Reverend Dr R Reusch, who worked for many years in the Kilimanjaro area. Reusch climbed Kilimanjaro about 50 times, the first being in 1926, when he became only the ninth known person to do so since Meyer and Purtscheller in 1889. It was Reusch who had discovered the frozen leopard, cutting off an ear as a memento after attempting, unsuccessfully, to cut off the whole head.

It is, perhaps, there also that King Menelik I and his slaves went to die, taking with them King Solomon's seal and other treasures. But the jewels of Kibo are to be found in its gleaming crystals of snow and fantastic fields of ice, encrusted with diamonds of light, clear and pure and sharp. And the jewels are being stolen, not so much by the sun, for flat faces of ice reflect much of the solar radiation, but, paradoxically, by the shadows, where radiant energy can more easily be absorbed. Everywhere the ice is in retreat. In the last quarter of the 19th century annual precipitation on the peaks decreased considerably. That was followed, in the first half of the 20th century, by a rise in average temperatures amounting to a few degrees centigrade. Those climatic changes have obviously affected the Kilimanjaro ice-cap in recent times but represent, to some extent, longer term cycle trends in glaciation.

During the Pleistocene, the glaciers on Kilimanjaro might have reached down to about 3,000 metres, the altitude at which the present rainforest merges into the heath. The mountain is beautiful now – how must it have looked then? But as late as the end of the 19th century Hans Meyer recorded that a continuous ice wall existed on the eastern rim of Kibo. Much of that area is now free of ice for, as on all the other high mountains of East Africa, the glaciers are receding. Those on Kibo's southern flanks, named after prominent Germans by early explorers, have already lost their definition, with the exception of the Heim Glacier which still retains its distinct shape. The so-called 'Southern Icefield', of which the Heim is a part, is now separated from the remnants of the Ratzel Glacier on Kibo's eastern rim. And the Ratzel itself is disintegrating rapidly into separate entities. Similarly, in the Kibo crater itself and in the area of the Western Breach, the ice is diminishing. Only the 'Northern Ice Field' on the north-west slopes of the peak survives as a large, continuous body of ice.

This great northern glacier is a radiant wonderland, a terraced hierarchy of ice, the vertical face of each step fluted into irregular columns and buttresses as if chiselled by imaginative master craftsmen. In fact the sculpting is largely caused

Opposite: Africa's great white mountain silhouetted against the rising sun.

by exposure to the equatorial sun traversing in arcs which are, for much of the day, directly or almost directly overhead. Some of these ornamented cliffs tower to a height of 30 metres, the ice a pale, translucent green when penetrated by light, elsewhere a slightly creamy white infused in places with subtle blues. But everywhere intricately carved or dimpled or hung with slender spines of ice, gleaming with meltwater or frozen into the cold grey shadows.

The vertical rays of the tropical sun, together with the dry air, are also responsible for similarly intricate sculptures among the Kilimanjaro snow-fields, though on a much smaller scale. The fields are melted into a tussocky texture composed of irregular spikes of hardened snow, sharp-edged and shaped into forms resembling hands, clasped in prayer. Hence the phenomenom's Spanish name, (*nieve de los penitentes*). And the sun's movements are the cause of a noticeable east-west asymmetry in the Kibo ice-fields. The glaciers of the western slopes descend to around 4,800 metres, a thousand metres lower down the mountain than the glaciers of the eastern rim.

The eternal snows of Kilimanjaro are, sadly, not eternal and the melting snow and ice is not being replaced as quickly as it is disappearing. Precipitation at the summit is only about 12 cm a year, about one tenth of the annual rainfall in the forest and, ironically, most of the snow of Kibo peak falls 'upwards' as it is brought from below on the wind currents. In certain years, and at certain seasons, the White Mountain seems to live up to its name even now. But the truth is that Kibo, in the not-too-distant future, might be bare. A century after Hans Meyer first marvelled at the icy 'spectacle of imposing majesty and unapproachable grandeur', the ice and the grandeur are diminished. But the imposing majesty remains and, for most people, the easiest and most pleasant way to appreciate it (if ease and pleasure can be used to describe an arduous hike) is to walk to the top via the long-established Marangu Route, or the little-known but increasingly popular trails which lead up the mountain's southern slopes, or across the Shira Plateau, all of which are extremely scenic and less crowded.

Right: Dramatic ice formations on the rugged walls of the Breach.

Walking the White Mountain

The major trekking routes on Kilimanjaro

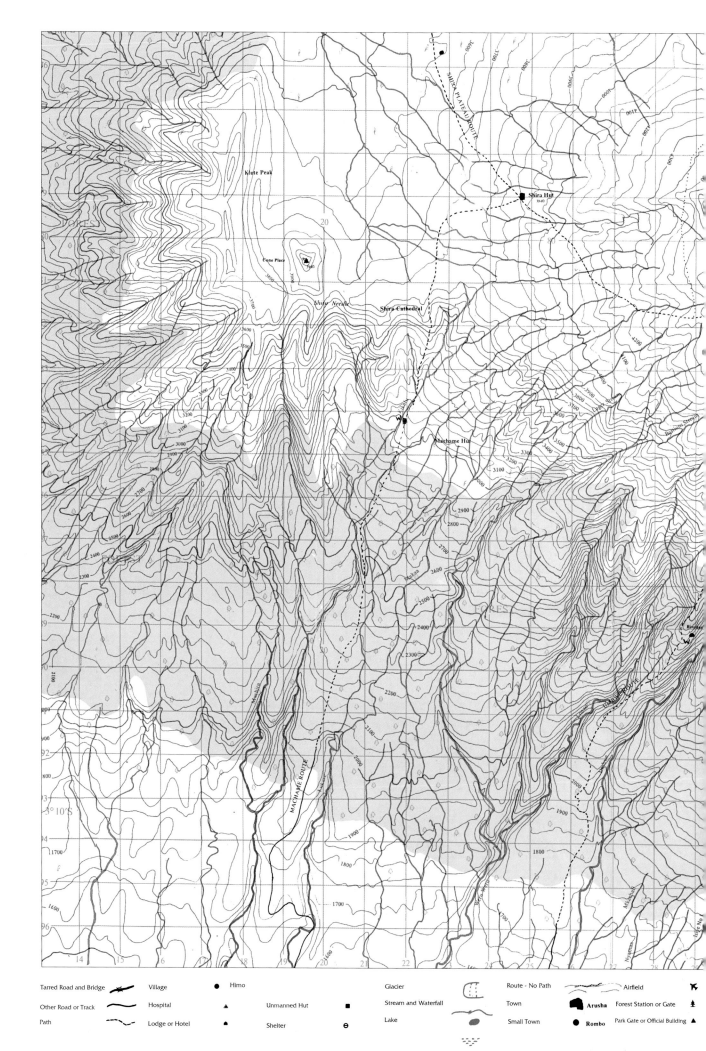

Klute Peak

Cone Place

Shira Needle

Shira Cathedral

Shira Hut

SHIRA PLATEAU ROUTE

Machame Hut

MACHAME ROUTE

3°10'S

Tarred Road and Bridge | Village | ● Himo | Glacier | Route - No Path | Airfield
Other Road or Track | Hospital | ▲ Unmanned Hut | ■ Stream and Waterfall | Town | **Arusha** | Forest Station or Gate
Path | Lodge or Hotel | ▲ Shelter | ⊖ Lake | Small Town | **Rombo** | Park Gate or Official Building

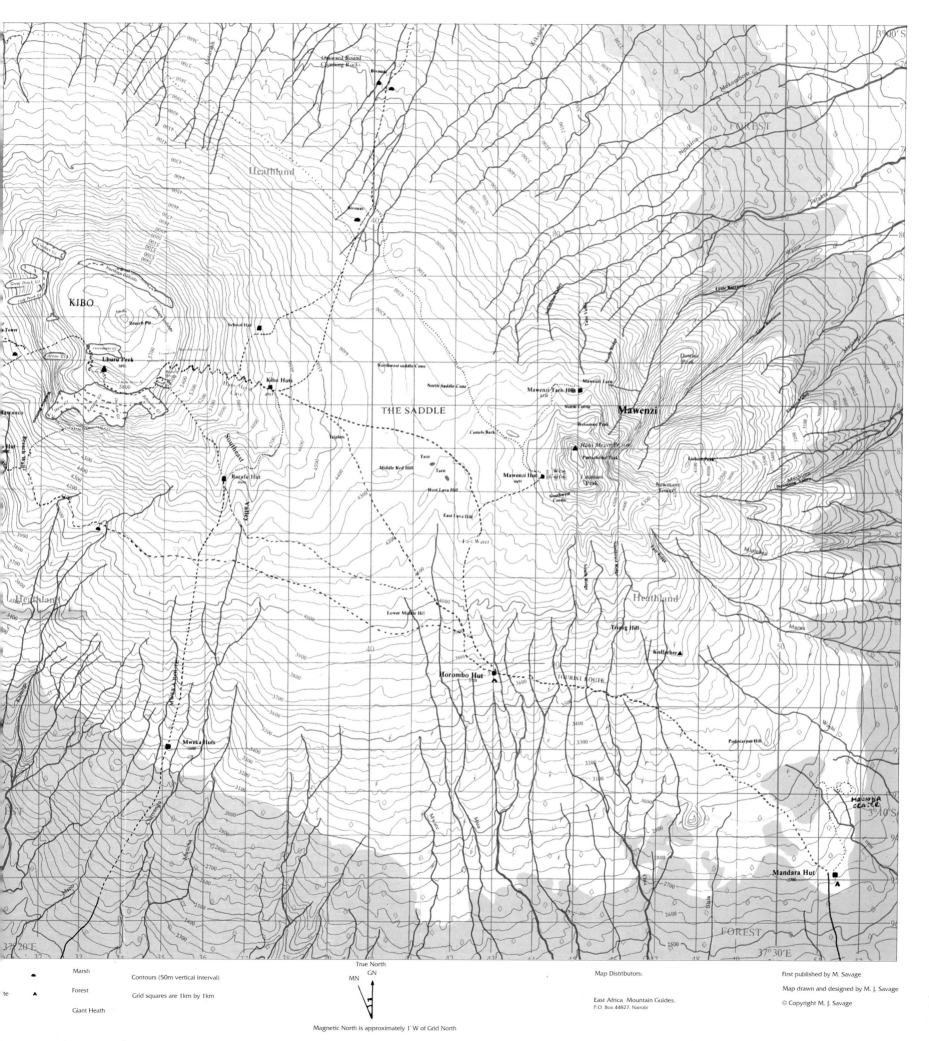

Marsh

Forest

Giant Heath

Contours (50m vertical interval)

Grid squares are 1km by 1km

True North
GN

MN

Magnetic North is approximately 1° W of Grid North

Map Distributors:

East Africa Mountain Guides.
P.O. Box 44827, Nairobi

First published by M. Savage

Map drawn and designed by M. J. Savage

© Copyright M. J. Savage

KIBO

Uhuru Peak

Kibo Hut

THE SADDLE

Mawenzi

Mawenzi Tarn Hut

Mawenzi Hut

Barafu Hut

Horombo Hut

Mweka Huts

Mandara Hut

TOURIST ROUTE

Heathland

Heathland

FOREST

FOREST

School Hut

Bivouac

Marangu Trail: The 'Tourist Route'

There are a number of comfortable 'base camps' close to Kilimanjaro, ranging from simple hostels or guest houses to small or medium hotels, three of which are located around the village of Marangu near which this particular route up the mountain begins.

The oldest of these hotels is the Kibo which was established in 1910 and still retains the charm and ambience of its Teutonic origins. Its interior decor includes wall desplays of climbers' flags and pennants, Germanic heraldic crests, and photographs of Johannes Rebmann's birthplace and of Hans Meyer, all of which contribute to the hotel's nostalgic air of old colonial ease. The Marangu Hotel started as a farmhouse built by a Czechoslovakian immigrant, Martin von Lamy, in 1893. Whilst raising a family he experimented with various agricultural projects on his land and finally succeeded with his coffee plantation. In 1932 the coffee market slumped and, not to be defeated like other coffee growers around him, he converted his home into a guest house. Fortunately for von Lamy Kilimanjaro soon became ever more popular amongst walkers and climbers and his daughter, Erica, converted the original homestead into an attractive, extremely comfortable hotel which is still owned and managed by family descendants to this day. Just up the Marangu trail from the Kibo and Marangu hotels is the much more recently built Capricorn Hotel which combines both imagination and local materials in its design. The Capricorn might lack the decades-old charms that age and experience have lent to its nearby competitors but it is also a fine hotel in lovely surroundings. As its woodwork weathers with the years and its reputation is enhanced by events and personalities, it will no doubt attract its own faithful flock of regular clients.

The gateway of Kilimanjaro National Park, a short distance from Marangu village and which marks the official beginning and end of the standard five-day climb to Kibo peak (three days up, two days down), is 1,800 metres above sea level. The first stage of the ascent, which follows the Marangu Trail or 'Tourist Route', takes about three or four hours and ends at Mandara Hut, close to the upper edge of the rainforest at 2,700 metres. The track is rocky and in places a little steep, but it was built originally to take four-wheel drive traffic and the walk, for a reasonably fit person, is straightforward.

Probably 90% of the people who attempt to climb Kilimanjaro use this particular route. Which is why it is described in detail below, and why it is sometimes known as the 'Coca Cola Trail'. This epithet, incidentally, also acts as a dig at the amount of litter sometimes encountered on the 'Marangu', but the route is basically beautiful and enjoyable and deserves its popularity.

For those who feel sorry for themselves as they plod up through the forest, a moment's comparison with the passing porters will put things in perspective. The men (some of them hardly out of their boyhood) work on contract, and work isn't always easy to get. It certainly isn't easy to do. Porters are obliged to carry about 15 kilos but often agree to carry more, and even 15 kilos, when carried on the head as is usually the case, is heavy enough on the Kilimanjaro gradients. A train of porters threading their way up the track, loads on heads and simple shoes (if any) on their feet, is as close as many people get to the great foot caravans of old. To see these hardy men on the move, uncomplaining and sometimes singing as they stride out between the trees or across the moorland, is a humbling experience. For the five-day stint, porters are paid the equivalent of what many of their clients would spend on a single meal in a reasonable provincial restaurant. Guides and assistant guides get the equivalent of two such meals – or less.

The porters, like most Africans, rise early and it is advisable, in East Africa, to do likewise. Tropical Africa, on the

Opposite: Packing up camp in the forest at the beginning of the Umbwe route.

whole, is at its best in the early morning when the air is often cool and the light superb. At 2,000 metres the temperatures are usually gentle throughout the day, but in the Kilimanjaro forest rain is less likely in the morning, and birds more active. Not so many birds or animals are likely to be seen, for rainforest birding isn't always easy and the Marangu Trail is a disturbed one. But Hartlaub's turacos and a few other birds are sometimes in evidence, and Blue monkeys might be sighted as they feed among the nearby branches. Mostly, however, the animals are conspicuous by their absence.

Not so the trees. They, and their understorey, are the main feature of this first stage, enclosing the walker in a green gorge colonnaded by the trunks of the forest trees, large and small, straight and twisted, branched and unbranched. For most people this is their first experience of rainforest and it can be pleasantly misleading. Were they to step off the track to explore the prodigality of foliage and ferns they would, as likely as not, soon be brought to a standstill. Rainforests, might be worthy of the world's attention, and fascinating places, but they are possessive of their privacy.

The embranglement of leaves, branches and saplings, fallen trees, giant ferns and hanging, looping vines, frustrates or denies access to the casual intruder and limits the probing equatorial light. To those whose experience of tropical forests is superficial or second-hand, a short walk into the green and gloomy disorder soon confronts them with rainforest realities. The forest is not a beech-wood or a regimented plantation of pines or an extensive grove of birch in which to wander at will. By Amazonian standards the Kilimanjaro forest is small but it is still fairly large on an African scale, girdling the massive mountain, and the ongoing fight for light and life beneath its canopy has an African intensity. The intruder, standing among the shadows and struck dumb by the watchful silence of the forest, might feel that he has blundered into something he cannot comprehend, that the trees themselves, hearing his approach, have frozen motionless in mid-struggle to look upon him with a disturbing indifference.

Most people, for whatever reason, stick to the track where they can see the sky and other people and, if they are observant, familiar-looking plants such as clover, the African elderberry (Sambucus africanus), a raspberry and a bramble. The raspberry and blackberry belong to the genus Rubus, and are therefore members of the Rose family. They are distinguished by their white flowers resembling those of the wild rose, and of course by their prickles and fruit. There are less familiar flowers too, begonias and balsams and a high altitude Leonotis-mollissima. Like other members of its genus it is easily recognized by the vertical series of green, spiky balls from which the tubular orange flowers protrude. The generic name means 'lion's ear', an allusion to the velvety nature of the corolla.

For those who wish to compromise with the rainforest, there is a trail which leads off the main track which it rejoins about half-way to Mandara. It adds a little distance and incovenience to the walk but more interest and privacy, and gives visitors an insight into the lonely, chaotic beauty of the rainforest. If lunchtime coincides with this stage of the journey, the streamside path is a restful, pleasant place to picnic.

Another interesting way to occupy your time on the walk to Mandara, as with other stages of the climb, is to observe the gradual change in vegetation with increasing altitude. The approach to the complex of A-frame huts at Mandara (built by the Norwegians) is through clumps of giant heather, hung with lichens, before climbers emerge into the forest clearing where the huts are situated.

The main hut at Mandara was designed, it seems, with Scandanavian gregariousness in mind. It is like a large timber

Above: Directional signboards at Mandara hut.

barn of triangular section, its lower storey dedicated to dining (and sometimes carousing,) its upper storey reached by a small ladder and serving as a simple dormitory. In the evenings, as walkers dine at the long trestle tables along the side walls, the fug from a multitude of woollen-swathed bodies and the smoky heat of a wood-burning stove permeates the room and is exaggerated by the weak light of paraffin lamps. It is a scene into which a Viking longboat crew might wander without feeling out of place. Smaller A-frame cabins are scattered around the clearing as if the main hut had given multiple birth to facsimiles of itself. They offer more privacy, after dinner, to those unsociable races and individuals who prefer to sleep, at least, with people to whom they have been introduced.

For those walkers who have time and breath to spare at Mandara, a short hike through the adjacent forest will bring them to Maundi Crater. On the way they will see, by the path, the pretty little endemic balsam, *Impatients kilimanjari*, and if they are lucky, and at the right time of day, an equally attractive bird which is sometimes encountered there, the sparrow-sized Oriole finch (*Linurgis olivaceus*). The male is a deep golden yellow bird with a contrasting black head and throat further set off by an orange bill. In a shaft of sunlight and seen through binoculars, the colour combination is arresting.

Maundi Crater itself is a parasitic cone, a grass and shrub-covered amphitheatre, its rim rising to 3,050 metres. From this vantage point at the upper edge of the forest, there are good views, on a clear day, of Lake Chala, 27 kilometres away on the Tanzania/Kenya border. Just beyond it lies the town of Taveta, with the remnants of its welcoming woodland, where Joseph Thomson and so many other explorers and caravan leaders loved to linger, seduced by the lotus-eating lifestyle and the attractive girls.

There are no such distractions, as a rule, at Mandara, and after an early breakfast on the second day most walkers are keen to begin the next stage; to break out of the forest on to the heath and upland moors. Soon after skirting the base of Maundi Crater the track crosses a meadow and a wooded stream before emerging into the open heath and grassland. If the clouds have not yet formed over Kibo the snow-capped peak can then be seen and, in the clear light the intervening moorland can be telescoped with Kibo seeming deceptively close. Young and healthy walkers, intoxicated by the mountain air and their release from the constraints of the rainforest, might feel that they could race across the slopes to touch for themselves the famous snows.

But the snows are two days distant. Meanwhile, the walk across the moors is invigorating. There are interesting heaths and a variety of grasses and flowers, and the first of the giant lobelias which grow in these uplands, often with a scarlet-tufted sunbird or two clinging to their bracts as the birds seek out insects with their slender, decurved bills. The walk takes about five or six hours and it is well to remember old Erica's advice, 'slowly slowly', for as the track approaches the second complex of huts, Horombo, it crosses a series of small but frustrating ravines. The altitude then begins to take effect, for the huts, at 3,720 metres, are only 250 metres lower than the Eiger.

Horombo and the Eiger have little else in common. The huts are set in a rocky valley at the base of the Mawenzi lava dykes, often shrouded in mist, and populated by the monstrous giant groundsels which live in their tribal lands behind the huts among a spongy alpine bog. Beyond this lost world, above the lava cliffs at the head of the valley, the snow-touched spires of Mawenzi can sometimes be seen. Other distractions at Horombo are few unless you are engaged in the study of the Four-striped mouse, the Streaky seed-eater or the Alpine chat, or get your thrills from feeding scavenging ravens.

Above: *View of the mountain from a lower section the Umbwe route.*

A more common but less attractive alternative is to trek up and down to Horombo's much-frequented lavatories, perched rather precariously at the edge of a rocky spur. Were it possible to sit enthroned and look out to the south, much of sub-equatorial Africa would lie in splendour before the incumbent, and the toilet might earn renown as a tourist attraction. In reality, the enclosed wooden closet and the cold updrafts from below, combined with the incipient headaches and nausea caused by altitude, encourage constipation. Or at least the idea of constipation; at 3,720 metres, the bowels begin to lose their self-control.

It is said to be a good idea to spend an extra night at Horombo. It would seem to make sense in terms of acclimatisation, though this particular cure for altitude sickness can sometimes appear worse than the affliction. Horombo is higher than most walkers will have been in their lives, except in aircraft, and the altitude and the cold nights, when sleepers might experience strange dreams, their breathing interrupted by long pauses, do not encourage extended stop-overs. Many walkers choose to move on the next morning to even greater discomforts at the far end of the Saddle. This third stage, like the second, takes the average walker about five or six hours despite the fact that much of it, across the sway-back ridge, is over gentle gradients.

For those walkers whose constitutions can cope with altitude, the walk is pleasant. The first landmark, about one-and-a-half kilometres above Horombo, is a low cliff of dark lava banded by paler striations caused by water seepage. It is known as Zebra Rock. A little further on is the stream known as 'Last Water'. It is aptly named – all the surface water beyond it is locked in the frozen grip of the ice-fields. Walkers pausing by this stream might like to know that in June 1887 Teleki and von Hohnel had paused there too, on their way to their own particular ordeal, and that a few weeks after them Dr Hans Meyer had named the stream Schneequelle, 'Snow stream', as it bubbled, at that time, from a drift of snow. Modern climbers might be astonished to learn that Meyer encountered six-foot drifts of snow on the southern slopes of the Saddle.

Driving blizzards can still white out the barren landscape: a few years ago a porter died of exposure within ten minutes walk of Kibo Hut. But snow or not, there is something of a sense of triumph in reaching the Saddle and once there, fine views can be enjoyed of the west face of Mawenzi and, across the dipping desolation of the ridge, of Kibo's eastern screes topped with their terraces of ice. The very desolation of the Saddle, like the sterile beauty of certain deserts, can be appealing. But for those prone to altitude sickness, the sight of Kibo Hut across the gentle swing of the Saddle can be as cruel as a mirage. For them, the toil up the western rise of the Saddle, especially the last few kilometres, can be demoralising as their hearts thump blood around tired lungs and limbs, and the thumping and throbbing is amplified in the head.

It is there that nervous newcomers to the Kilimanjaro experience might gloomily recall the notices they would have seen, two days earlier, by the park gates. Describing the effects of altitude sickness and its most serious form, pulmonary oedema, these notices talk of '. . . a dry cough and blood-stained sputum, and bubbling noises in the chest'. This encouraging information is quickly followed (in case the reader is of a flippant disposition) by a chilling prophecy: 'Lips, tongue, nose, ears and fingernails turn blue. . . Without treatment, death quickly follows.'

Altitude sickness is, of course, a serious business, but in reality few people suffer anything worse than fairly unpleasant discomforts and death from any cause on Kilimanjaro is quite rare. Almost everyone who ascends to Horombo and beyond, however, will have to learn to live with nausea, headaches, stomach upsets, aching limbs and a

Above: Kibo hut, at the centre of the picture, is lost in the snow on the flanks of Kilimanjaro.

shortage of breath and energy. The difference in effect between particular individuals is one of degree rather than kind – the summit which they are trying to reach, after all, is 5,896 metres high.

Kibo Hut, the last outpost of civilisation before that decisive and drawn-out slog, has an altitude of 4,703 metres, almost the same as Mont Blanc, the highest peak in western Europe. But for most, the hike across the Saddle is followed by a pleasant enough afternoon lazing in the sun among the nearby rocks. Only the icy touch of a creeping shadow, in late afternoon, or a look at the scree slopes of Kibo through binoculars brings a mild and momentary touch of foreboding. But as darkness falls like the ice-cold blade of a guillotine, the prospect of dinner (often little more than lukewarm soup and bread) followed, at best, by a few hours restless sleep, is not a joyful one.

If Kibo Hut were situated in Paradise it would still be listed, in the angels' gazeteer of low-budget accommodation, as eminently uninviting. Four-and-three-quarter kilometres up on a bleak mountainside, and in the middle of the night, it is like a high-altitude open prison, at least to those inmates whose thresholds of discomfort were previously determined by the availability (or otherwise) of Dover sole in their favourite restaurant. Or some other such deprivation. These unfortunate souls (and we are many) toss and turn in their thick woollens and sleeping bags, stomachs churning and heads throbbing, waiting, almost praying, to get it all over with. Meanwhile ice forms, from condensation, on the concrete floor.

Napoleon Bonaparte regarded the rarest kind of courage as that which manifests itself at three o'clock in the morning. At Kibo Hut the call to action often comes two hours earlier. And even the Little Corsican would have agreed that to climb

153

Above: Kibo camp on a clear, sunny day.

out of a snug sleeping bag in the middle of the night in order to stagger up a steep and frozen scree slope, 1,200 metres high, is a rather odd thing to do. 1,200 metres is almost as high as Mount Vesuvius, but climbing Kibo peak from Kibo Hut is like climbing Vesuvius with one lung and with lead-soled boots while suffering from flu. It isn't fun.

But it is an unexpectedly moving experience and one which, in retrospect, most of those involved would not have missed. After playing a minor role for three days the guides and their assistants suddenly undergo a metamorphosis. These normally laconic, unassuming men remain laconic – every breath is gold-plated at these altitudes – but they wear, for the first time on the walk, an unmistakable authority. They also wear, again for the first time, anoraks, thickly-woven trousers and serious-looking head-gear and boots. They look like under-equipped but dauntless Marine commandos about to storm some Arctic stronghold. Which is pretty much what they are about to do.

Their platoons are a motley bunch. Members might represent one country or five or six. Some might be as fit and healthy as thoroughbred racehorses while others might have enjoyed a misspent youth (and middle-age) in bars and billiard halls and – who knows? – perhaps bordellos. A few will have experienced high altitude before but most will be learning how to vomit in a completely new environment. There will be the young, and not-so-young, male and female, fat and thin, the good, the bad and the ugly. And even the homogeneous neutrality of cold-climate clothing fails to unite them for people have climbed Kibo in flimsy plastic macs and old trainers, woolly cardigans knitted by long lost grannies, string vests and long johns, football socks and baseball caps and balaclavas. The more upmarket tourists will look like models for a Swiss mountain clothing catalogue, the rest as if they've just been dragged from the nearest Oxfam shop. But almost everyone will have a steel-tipped stick.

It is the tap, tap of the steel tips striking the scree which soon beats out the rhythm of the climb, extremity uniting the group of walkers, each with his or her own thoughts and private fears of failure, each conserving those most precious of commodities at altitude, energy and breath. Each party will shuffle up the shortening zig-zags of the track mostly in silence and in single file. At their head will be the guide dictating the pace, plodding through the darkness or the moonlight with a tiny paraffin lamp and sometimes singing a repetetive, doleful chant, a mantra to the mighty mountain. At the tail of the file will come, as a rule, his assistant, also with a lamp.

It makes sense, on a steep slope of scree, to 'tack' from side to side, but the broad zig-zags of the lower slopes of Kibo can be terribly demoralising, when heart-beats are pounding in heads, lungs are heaving for oxygen and legs are in slow motion. Many metres must be walked to gain a few. No one now needs to remember old Erica's 'Pole, Pole!' – 'Slowly, slowly!'. Time, like legs, seems to be moving through an intense gravitational field. Walkers begin to focus, mindlessly, on the boots of the person ahead, plodding trance-like to the next elbow of a zig-zag where the guide will call a momentary halt to replenish the lungs and give his troops a little pep talk. Then off on the next arm of the zig-zag with a slow and deliberate tap, tap, tap of the steel-tipped sticks.

The zig-zags shorten, height is somehow gained, step by heavy step, and after two hours or so the Hans Meyer Cave, a large overhang about half-way to the crater rim, is reached. Parties sometimes rest in the icy darkness of the cave to gulp down water or fruit juice. At over 5,000 metres dehydration is a serious threat. Such a cave, perhaps, gave rise to the story told to Johannes Rebmann by his guide. The guide claimed that he had met a man called Sabaya, the sole survivor of a large expedition that had been appointed by a local king to examine the mysterious white material that covered Kibo. Despite the deaths of all his companions, Sabaya had pressed on until he reached a large open door studded with iron spikes. Too weak and frightened to enter, and suffering badly from crippling frostbite, he had retreated. Could it be possible that the 'open door' was the Hans Meyer Cave, its entrance spiked, as it still often is, with icicles?

Guides will not allow walkers to rest for long on Kibo. The shortage of oxygen combined with weariness from lack of sleep and three days of fairly rigorous walking can induce a seductive drowsiness. Without wasting too many words, guides will soon have their platoon back on its weary feet, and labouring up the steepening scree between ice-cold rocks. Above the cave the narrow path makes short but more regular switchbacks, and anyone foolish enough to glance at a watch will find that its fingers have frozen. Or so it will seem.

But at last, for those who have managed to keep going, dawn begins to lighten the skies behind them over the invisible Mawenzi. Daybreak itself seems to unravel as slowly as a flower and the hypnotic rhythm of the walkers' steps, and their regular, constant halts for breath, is not affected. Then suddenly the rhythm and the trance is broken, for the last part of the climb is a scramble through and over the rocks to Johannes Notch and, just above it to the left, Gillman's Point. There is, for most climbers, little elation. Just relief and an overwhelming desire to get to the crater rim and collapse. There is no charge of adrenalin to boost exhausted leg muscles and power them up the last fifty metres or so of rock, only a mechanical, almost involuntary shuffle, forwards and upwards, until the group finds itself standing, or sitting, or even lying, at the top of Africa. . .

. . . Almost. For like Hans Meyer and Ludwig Purtscheller more than a century before they find that the top of Africa, two hundred and ten metres higher and another hour-and-a-half's weary walk away, taunts them from along the crater rim away to the west. Africa is a tolerant continent, and 210 metres is neither here nor there when you are standing at Gillman's Point with legs like concertinas and a head that threatens to explode. And besides, the earth, the restless earth which created this awful but compelling mountain, is turning now towards the sun. At these heights, half-way to the stratosphere, the moments before sunrise, as experienced air travellers will know, can be startlingly different from those at lower levels.

Dramatically primitive skies, almost from the blackness of space through indigo and ultramarine, lined at their lighter edge with cobalt and cerulean, can be fired through with isolated bars of vermilion or deep orange. There are no clouds to obscure or soften, and only half an atmosphere to filter the ultra violet. The light is unequivocal, the colours raw, violent in their simplicity. The sort of sky that a mountain like Kilimanjaro deserves. And the sort of sky that those who struggle up to Gillman's Point deserve to witness.

As the sun rises, silhouetting the shattered peaks of Mawenzi – often an island in a sea of foaming, flocculent cloud – its low-angled rays strike the snows and terraces of ice on Kibo and flood the crater with light and shadow. It doesn't cure mountain sickness, or aching legs, but those who stand at Gillman's Point will never forget those moments. And as they take a last photograph, or not-so-lingering look, and gratefully set off down the scree with every stride taking them nearer to normality and comfort, the exhilaration begins to mount and the adrenalin, at last, to flow. They have walked the great White Mountain.

*Above: Climbers headlamps snake through the snow
o Gilman's Point in July.

Above: The view from Gillman's Point as the sun rises behind Mawenzi.

Right: View of the mountain across the rocky surface of the Shira Plateau.

The Shira Route

There are other walks on Kilimanjaro, the easiest and in many ways the most satisfying being across the Shira Plateau which begins at Londorossi Glades to the west of Kibo. To get there, you must take the main Arusha-Moshi road and turn off at Boma la Ng'ombe (Hai) to West Kilimanjaro. After 23 km the tarred road gives way to dirt which traverses – for a further 20 km – a deep-stream valley. At this point you will come to a fork, where you bear right on to a forestry road which leads uphill for 13 km to the park gate at Londorossi. It is important to keep your eyes peeled for the signpost to the gate as it is easy, in Londorossi, to take the wrong track. About 19 km from the gate, once you have found it, there is a good campsite by a stream, with a rock shelter. Beyond the campsite the track continues for about three kilometres across a saddle between Shira Dome and the western slopes of Kibo at an altitude of about 3,740 metres.

The route, which of course approaches Kilimanjaro from the opposite direction to that of the Marangu Route, is partly motorable in four-wheel drive though extremely rugged in places. From Londorossi it rises through three kilometres of forest, reaching heathland at 2,600 metres before emerging on to the edge of the Plateau. Which is, perhaps, the most enchanting of Kilimanjaro's many-splendoured attractions, its rolling moorland rising gently towards the striking severity of Kibo's Breach Wall and its flanking glaciers.

The gentleness of the Plateau can mislead visitors, especially those who have driven rather than walked from Londorossi to the roadhead, into thinking that it is easier than it looks. The walk to the Plateau is relatively undemanding but, when a vehicle is used, the rapid gain in altitude can lead to the equally rapid onset of mountain sickness. Would-be climbers arriving at the roadhead in this way are well advised to spend one or two extra days on the Shira before attempting anything higher.

The Shira Hut is the only reasonably permanent accommodation in the immediate vicinity but readers should remember that situations change even as books like this are being written. Shira Hut, like certain other huts on the mountain's less frequently used routes, is old and not too clean, and many parties prefer to camp, in this case by Shira Cave, twenty minutes' walk south-south-east of the hut. In any case hikers, if they are organising their own climb, should always try to ascertain the latest developments especially with regard to accommodation, before embarking on their trek. Shira Hut, for those who do wish to use it, comprises a single uniport structure intended to house a maximum of eight people and water is available from a stream 165 feet (50 metres) from Shira Hut or from a stream ten minutes' walk from Shira Cave. A wooden lavatory stands by the cave itself.

The hut is only about half an hour's walk from the roadhead but, at almost 12,500 feet (3,800 metres) it is higher than Horombo, the second hut on Marangu Route, and the altitude, though in no way threatening, should be treated with respect. Extra days on the Shira, however, are usually a pleasure rather than a penance. Unless the weather is unusually severe just being on the Plateau is rewarding and relaxing. More active walkers can explore its southern and western edges, from the landmarks known as the East Shira Hill, the Shira Cathedral and Shira Needle to Klute Peak on the Shira Ridge. The peaks known as the Cathedral and Needle are particularly dramatic. And of course you don't need to be an expert botanist or ornithologist to enjoy the plants and birds of these upland heaths and moors. Larger mammal species, as elsewhere on the mountain, are not too often in evidence though eland inhabit the plateau, lions sometimes range through, and the spoor of leopard and buffalo might sometimes be observed.

Opposite: Porters enjoying the warm of the cooking fire in their cave at the Shira Plateau camp.

Machame Route

The Marangu ascent described earlier has become known, rather disparagingly and rather unfairly, as the 'Coca Cola Route' because of its popularity. The trail beginning in Machame has now acquired the equally inappropriate epithet 'The Whisky Route', presumably to distinguish it from its more egalitarian counterpart. Though this name alludes to the greater expenses involved, as well as the route's more intoxicating views, those attempting to ascend it are advised not to hit the bottle.

The Machame is the westernmost of three more or less parallel routes rising directly up the southern slopes of Kibo, each named after the village from which it starts. The Machame is the only one of the three regarded as a genuine ascent and eventually links with the Shira Route at the Shira Hut. It is regarded by many as the most beautiful of all approach trails to Kibo peak. When combined with the Barafu Route to the summit it has perhaps the highest rate of success of all the routes on the mountain, mostly due to the slowness of the ascent.

The initial climb through the rainforest is relatively gradual, though at times progress may be hampered by slippery conditions and/or fallen trees. Reasonablly fit and determined walkers, however, will find little to worry them and their efforts will be rewarded, upon their emergence on the edge of the Shira Plateau, by excellent views of the southern glaciers.

To access this route, you travel west from Moshi along the main Moshi-Arusha road for about 13 kilometres before turning right towards Machame Village, a further seven kilometres. If you are travelling by private car, it should be possible to leave it at the hotel or the school just prior to entering Machame. You then continue on foot for a little over one kilometre into Machame itself. Continue for almost three kilometres through coffee farms and forest to the Park gate, an undemanding two hour walk from Machame.

The track from here continues through plantation and then indigenous forest before rising through heath and moorland along a well-used and clearly defined ridge, with Weru Weru Stream below you to the east and Makoa Stream to the west. Two hours or so from the Park gate, you should reach the trailhead. Four or five hours of more walking, along a narrow path, should then bring you to Machame Huts, south-west of Kibo and about two-and-a-half kilometres south of Shira Hut. The Machame Huts (there are two uniports, each housing six people) are a little below the edge of the plateau at 9,850 feet (3,000 metres). At the time of writing (1999) they are in a state of disrepair. Water is always available from a stream five minutes walk down the steep hill to the north-west, and fuel is said to be plentiful. Basic lavatories are provided.

The second day's ascent, which takes about five hours, brings those involved to the Shira Hut area. Above Machame Hut the trail emerges on to the moorland, crossing a valley and continuing up a steep ridge of volcanic rock. A semi-circular rock wall, about two hours above the huts, has to be negotiated by scrambling but it is very short and, for the average hiker, straightforward. Beyond the wall there is a rest stop for those who choose to make use of it, with fine views of the mountain scenery. The trail then turns away from Kibo, heading north-west and crossing two stream valleys before rising to Shira Hut.

Many people intending to climb to Uhuru Peak link up with the South Circuit Route from Shira, travelling eastwards below Kibo to Barafu Hut and thence to the summit. These possibilities are described later.

Above: A crude signboard marks the start of the Machame route.

Umbwe Route

The Umbwe Route is a relatively short but steep route which eventually joins the Southern Circuit at Barranco Hut. Cameron Burns, mountaineering author of the very useful climbing and trekking guide, *Kilimanjaro and Mount Kenya*, describes it as 'easily one of the best experiences of a lifetime'. He also describes it, without apparent irony, as 'breathtaking', and as he goes on to say that it is 'wild, rough and extremely steep' one can assume that one's breath is not just abducted by the glory of the scenery. The scenery is undoubtedly superb offering views, from the moorland, of the Southern Icefields and the Breach Wall. Surprisingly few people presently use the route and most of those that do choose to come down it rather than go up, both because of its steeper incline and the fact that permits are not issued at the Umbwe Gate. In the interests of consistency, however, the route is described here from bottom to top.

About four miles (almost six-and-a-half kilometres) west of Moshi there is a right turn leading to Weru Weru. Some seven miles (eleven kilometres) beyond Weru Weru, on the Lyamungu Road, you will come to a T-junction leading towards Mango. Turn right at the junction and proceed until you cross a bridge over a small river, soon after which (about 150 metres) you turn left to Umbwe Mission where you may leave your vehicle.

There are no huts on the Umbwe Trail until you reach the Barranco (which is sometimes known as Umbwe Hut). Instead there are caves known prosaically as Camp (or Bivouac) One (Forest Caves) and Camp (or Bivouac) Two (Upper Caves). Camp One, an all-weather shelter with water close at hand and plentiful fuel (it is within the upper forest margins), is reached after a hike of four to six hours from the Mission along a former forestry track and, later, up a path along the narrow ridge which separates the Lonze and Umbwe Rivers (to west and east respectively). It is sometimes necessary to pull yourself up by means of tree roots and branches. The cave is at an altitude of 9,240 feet (2,800 metres).

Depending when you leave the Mission, you will either overnight at Camp one or continue to Camp Two, a rock overhang some three hours further up the trail in steep, open country. On the way to this second camp, at around 3,200 metres, you will encounter a short rock cliff which demands a little easy scrambling. Camp Two has limited water – there are springs 15 minutes down the ravine to the west or 990 feet (300 metres) down on the east side of the ridge. Above Camp Two the track continues along the ridge to Barranco Hut, a walk of only about two hours.

Mweka Trail

The third and easternmost track of the southern slopes trio, Mweka, leads to a less spectacular prospect and while being the steepest of Kilimanjaro's routes up the lower slopes, it is the most direct way of walking to the summit. More conveniently it is a quick way down!. It has the other advantage, for those based in Moshi Town, of beginning at Mweka, only nine miles or so (fifteen kilometres) north of the township though permits for the walk, as at Umbwe, cannot be obtained at Mweka Gate. Despite its greater popularity as a descent route, it will be decribed 'bottom up' rather than 'top down'.

The Trail begins at the Mweka College of Wildlife Management which is well signposted from the roundabout on the main Moshi-Arusha Road, on the northern outskirts of Moshi. The College, incidentally, has a good international reputation and, if you ask politely, the authorities there will allow you to leave your vehicle in the car park.

From the College you travel up an old logging track which can be quite slippery until, after about two hours, the track becomes a path, quite uneven in places and often muddy. The path rises steeply along a ridge through the forest just beyond which,s approximately six to eight hours hike from the College, stand the Mweka Huts. They are two furnished uniports, each intended for 8 people, and water and fuel are plentiful though there are no lavatories. The water source, a stream in a small valley five minutes to the south-east of the huts, is the last available water on the Mweka. The altitude here is 9,900 feet (3,000 metres).

The following day's hike takes you up the ridge to the west of the South East Valley. At about 14,100 feet (4,300 metres) you will cross the Southern Circuit Route and approximately one mile (just over one-and-a-half kilometres) further north of this point you will reach Barafu Huts, another two uniports housing eight persons each. *Barafu*, which means 'ice' in Swahili, is appropriately named as it stands at 15,100 feet (4,600 metres), below the Rebmann and Ratzel Glaciers. Water and fuel are not available, nor are there any lavatories. The walk from Mweka Huts to Barafu takes about six to eight hours.

Rongai Route

This route is currently the only standard route up Kilimanjaro's northern slopes. It takes its name from the village of Rongai which is situated on the Tanzanian side of the border with Kenya. Its Kenyan counterpart is the settlement of Oloitokitok and in the days of the old East African Community the route, quite well used at the time, was in fact known as the Loitokitok and is sometimes still referred to as such. The route, whichever name is used, is very different from other trails on the mountain. It is drier, there are no huts, and its relatively gentle slopes are covered in long grass and evidence of elephant. Sometimes the elephants themselves might be seen, which adds extra zest to the hike. There are fine views, also, across the Maasai plains beyond the border.

There needs to be some extra incentive: getting to Rongai requires driving fifty kilometres around the mountain from Marangu on an adventurously rough road. Travellers should turn right at the Marangu Post Office then circumnavigate the entire eastern massif, passing through a series of small but interesting villages. On the north-eastern slopes, at Tareka Village, you will find yourself close to a border post with Kenya. Aproaching the post itself, you take the Rongai Road which leads off to the left just before the gate. A little less than fifteen kilometres later you should arrive in Rongai.

Before setting off on the trek itself you must report to the Park gate, up the road to the left a short distance from Rongai. Then you must drive back down to the town and continue counter-clockwise around the mountain for several kilometres to a starting point to the left of the road and presently marked by a large white metal sign announcing 'Snow-Cap Mountain Climbing Camp – Rongai'. Such signs, and such establishments do not always last for long in Africa, and would-be hikers must be aware of this and use their common sense.

From this point the trail follows an old four-wheel-drive track as it winds upwards through the forest. After about one-and-a-half kilometres, at 8,200 feet (2,500 metres), it reaches the heath which it traverses with refreshing ease. This is attractive open country, richly manured with elephant droppings. At about 9,446 feet (2,880 metres) you will come across the so-called First Cave where most walkers camp for the night (there are very good campsites just above the cave, with beautiful panoramic views across the plains to the north). Water is available just below the cave, and there is a simple lavatory. There is also a wooden picnic table with benches.

The following day's route takes hikers towards Kibo, passing Second Cave on the way and reaching Third Cave where most parties on the Rongai take their second night's rest at 12,710 feet (3,875 metres). There is a stream below the cave and some more simple lavatories.

About twenty minutes' walk west of the Third Cave, the North Circuit Path (see below) leads off to the right in a northerly direction. There is also a trail that leads to Mawenzi Tarn Hut but it isn't easy to locate. From the Third Cave the track to Kibo Hut (on the popular Marangu Route) is fairly straightforward, traversing the northwestern shoulder of the Saddle between Mawenzi and Kibo.

Southern Circuit Route

More routes on Kibo, other than the Marangu, involve the Southern Circuit Route to some extent. It half-encircles Kibo on the peak's southern slopes and the scenery, as one might imagine even from the glance at a good map, is quite splendid. The route is well marked and going from west to east (which is the most common approach) takes in the Shira, Lava Tower and Barranco Huts, as well as the Barafu and Marangu Routes.

The trail begins (assuming you start in the west) on the Shira Plateau, just to the east of the intersection of the Northern and Shira Circuit paths, and to the east of a rock bearing, in red spray paint, the legend 'Moya Hut', the Kiswahili version of 'Moir'. This point is not always easy to find even now, and as the spray paint succumbs to the vagaries of high altitude weather, is hardly likely to get easier to locate. Many parties are said to miss it but none have actually gone missing altogether, and they all seem to home in on the Southern Circuit eventually and without too much stress.

Having found the intersection, walkers follow the trail down a rocky slope and bypass the Lava Tower to the south. This trail joins the Barranco Hut-Lava Tower route. The junction, on a ridge, is well marked, and two hours of easy hiking down the valley to the east will bring trekkers to the vicinity of the Barranco Hut which has evolved into an area rather than a specific location – there is a camp site close to the Southern Circuit Route but the actual hut is ten minutes' walk down the Great Barranco Valley, on its western slopes. Two small valleys have to be crossed to reach it.

The Barranco Valley, of course, is the ravine that was formed by the landslide which, some 100,000 years ago, caused the Great Breach. The next leg of the circuit takes hikers across it, confronting them, after crossing a stream at the valley bottom, with a very steep looking wall of rock 300 metres high. The wall is nothing like as daunting as it might seem to novices, as the paths zig-zag up it in a series of easily negotiated steps, a staircase through some pretty dramatic scenery up to a plateau of high alpine desert.

It is from the crest of the wall that those climbers intending to reach Kibo summit by way of the southern glacier routes branch off, up a track well defined by cairns. This book is not intended as a climbing guide, and readers requiring such information are advised to consult the books on Kilimanjaro and Mount Kenya by Iain Allen and Cameron Burns.

However, it is worth noting in passing that although the Southern Glaciers should not deter experienced climbers, they are melting back and changing form so that easy climbing today might be quite difficult climbing in the future. There are crevasses, too, to look out for, and Cameron Burns warns climbers of the massive seracs formed by the glaciers which, in the heat of the late morning, 'should be avoided . . . (they may calve off and crush you)'.

Lesser mortals who choose to stick to the Southern Circuit Route have no such worries though they are still able to share, at a safe distance, some of the technical climber's cherished privileges, for the route takes them beneath the same radiantly beautiful icefalls named, from west to east, the Heim, Kersten, Decken and Rebmann. Iain Allen (and mountaineers are known for their understatement) describes the Southern Circuit Route as 'perhaps the most spectacular trek on Kilimanjaro'. I doubt that many of those who follow in his footsteps would disagree.

From the eastern heights to the Barranco Valley the track, to the relief of those whose legs are feeling a bit rubbery after the ascent of the rock wall, gradually loses altitude though a series of small but energy-sapping valleys await them, the last of them deeper than the rest with a stream running through it. This water, incidentally, is the last for many kilometres. Not too far to the east of this valley the Southern Circuit Route crosses the Mweka on a ridge and the Barafu Hut (this

Opposite: Climbers enjoying breakfast in front of the Lava Tower.

route is described later) stands little more than one kilometre above the intersection.

Those people going on to join the main Marangu Route continue east, as one might expect, until the tracks meet on the Saddle not much more than a kilometre to the north-west of Horombo Hut. The hut – or group of huts – is of course much better than any of the huts encountered on the route so far, and will be a welcome sight for those arriving from Barranco, for the day's trek, while not particularly challenging for anyone who is reasonably fit, is still a fairly long hike at this altitude. Incidentally, for those who decide to walk this leg from east to west, the start of the Southern Circuit Route, just above Horombo, isn't always easy to find. The thing to look out for, at the time of writing (1999) is a small wooden sign saying merely 'Saddle' (as if its creator didn't have the energy or breath to write much else). The South Circuit track takes off just behind the sign.

Northern Circuit Route

Strictly speaking, this sub-title should read 'Western and Northern Sector' but for simplicity's sake it has been left as it is. Few parties actually use the route at present and until it is developed most people will prefer to stick to its southern counterpart, with its incomparable and often sunlit snow scenes and its more accessible approach routes and offshoots. It has, however, considerable potential, and is described here as a continuation of the Southern Circuit, setting off from Kibo Hut on the Marangu Route to pass counter-clockwise below Kibo peak's northern flanks.

The route, from Kibo to Moir (the only hut on the Northern Circuit) can be achieved in one day, but it is a long hard slog and an overnight bivouac to break the journey is advisable. As the trail passes just above the Third Cave on the Rongai Route, and as the cave constitutes the only shelter on the mountain's northern slopes, this might be considered as a possible extra stop-over. More adventurous parties might pitch camp elsewhere.

Whatever the case, the track along the northern slopes crosses a whole series of rock ribs and gullies, though it maintains an altitude of about 14,000 feet (4,300 metres) throughout most of its length, bringing walkers beneath the magnificent Northern Icefields to Moir Hut which is rather less magnificent. Cameron Burns describes it as yet another 'unappealing metal shell'. It was intended to accommodate 10 people, and stands at 13,800 feet (4,200 metres) in the Lent Valley, a little over a mile (2 kilometres) west of a prominent cluster of secondary cones known as the Lent Group. Water is limited at Moir, and fuel is not normally available. It is not a place to contemplate spending one's honeymoon, though privacy is fairly easy to come by. And to parties who have made a full day's hike, this particular 'unappealing metal shell' will seem no worse than many doss houses at sea level.

The last leg of the circuit, or more correctly a western extension of it starts next morning with an hour's walk or thereabouts from Moir to the intersection with the Shira Trail. This lies due west of the Oehler Ridge which projects westwards from beneath the Credner, Drygalski and Pengalski Glaciers. Beyond the intersection the track passes beneath the face of the Western Breach to Barranco Hut some four or five hours later. The Umbwe Route could then, for those wanting to leave the mountain the next day, be used as a descent.

Opposite: Mawenzi enshrouded in cloud as the sun rises behind it.

Alternative Hiking Routes to the Crater Rim

Approximately 90% of the people who reach Uhuru Point or the rim of the crater do so via the Marangu Route. This has been described earlier in full. There are, however, two alternatives for the non-specialist climber. These are the Barafu Route and the Western Breach Route.

The Barafu Route is the easier of the two. It is basically a continuation of the Mweka Route and is sometimes known as such. It begins at Barafu Hut to the north-west of Horombo at 4,600 metres.

The ascent from Barafu is direct and very steep, leading to the Rebmann Glacier at 16,071 feet (4,870 metres). Here you pass a cliff and proceed through the gap between the Rebmann and the Ratzel, arriving at the crater rim just west of Stella Point, (5,795 metres) some six hours after leaving Barafu and a further hour's walk from Uhuru Point. If following the same route down care must be taken to find the right gap between the two glaciers.

As suggested earlier, the Mweka, like the Umbwe, is more likely to be used as a descent route but, for those who know what they are doing and are fit and healthy, it provides a quick and direct path to the summit and back. The scenery is not quite so dramatic as it is from further west but it is still attractive, with extensive views (weather permitting!) over the plains, as well as the obvious panoramas of the mountain itself.

The Great Western Breach Route has an undeserved reputation among amateurs for being difficult but, although it calls for a little more effort and care than Marangu or Barafu, it is no more than a strenuous walk with a little easy scrambling at times. It is accessed from the vicinity of Lava Tower Hut, named after the main geological feature of the locality which arises nearby, on the edge of the Great Barranco and beneath the Western Breach. Like the tower of lava itself, the hut has been exposed to the ravages of time though with rather less interesting results. It is little more than a ruin, at an altitude of 15,180 feet (4,600 metres), where is, at least, available water but no lavatories.

Some two hours walk above it lie the ruins of another hut, the Arrow Glacier (which – just to inspire you – was partly destroyed by a falling rock). From this point the summit of Kibo can be reached via the Great Western Notch on the Crater rim. The route is very steep and although no actual climbing is involved it must be treated with respect. It follows a natural lava staircase through a gap in 'otherwise rotten' cliffs. This 'staircase' (composed of what Iain Allen, in that invaluable little *Guide to Mount Kenya and Kilimanjaro*, calls 'atrocious scree') is something of a scramble at times and needs to be ascended (and descended if necessary) with particular care. Further scrambling is necessary higher up and, while the glaciers can be bypassed, an ice-axe might prove handy on the snowfields which at certain times of year cover the entire Breach.

The route emerges on the crater rim just north of Furtwangler Glacier, at the western foot of the central ash cone. Iain Allen estimates that at least four hours are needed to get from Lava Tower Hut to Uhuru Point, but less serious climbers are advised to err on the side of caution. With this is mind, anyone planning to return by the same route on the same day should remember that the journey will take up most, if not all, of the available daylight. To avoid being caught in darkness on the steep descent it is advisable to start out from Lava Tower well before dawn. In any case, the Breach tends to fill with cloud later in the day and a compass (and/or a guide who is intimately familiar with the route) would be a welcome asset.

This precautionary tone with regard to the Great Western Breach Trail is necessary but it is not meant to deter the more adventurous travellers, providing they use their common sense and are in good physical condition. It isn't the easiest

way to the summit but the rewards are considerable. Apart from offering splendid views of the impressive Western Breach the route affords more immediate access to the remarkable Northern Icefields (though anyone contemplating such an extension of their trek should consult professional guides and make proper arrangements). Its point of emergence at the crater rim is also within a kilometre (a one hour walk at this altitude) of the inner (Reusch) Crater, with its associated Inner Cone, Terrace, Ash Pit and fumaroles.

The Inner Crater

Those people interested in visiting the Inner Crater should plan to include it in their itinerary before setting off, and should, of course, arrange everything beforehand with the National Park authorities, or their travel company and guide. The extra time and effort involved makes it advisable to concentrate on one thing or the other (either Uhuru Point or the Inner Crater) rather than try to attempt both in the same morning. Many people might be loath to give up the chance of standing at the highest point in Africa after coming so far but a trip to the Inner Crater is in its way much more interesting and just as exciting. For those ambitious and hardy souls who actually want to stand at Uhuru Point and in the Crater, and who are more comfortable than most at these oxygen-deficient heights, an alternative is to bivouac overnight in the Crater itself. This, of course, is not something to be taken lightly, not because it is intriniscally difficult or dangerous, but because of the altitude and climate. Once again, those interested should discuss possibilities with local experts before embarking on their trek.

Above: Looking across the Ruesch Pit.

Above: An aerial view of Kilimanjaro's summit.

Mawenzi and Mawenzi Tarn

Walkers wanting to get a closer look at Mawenzi have two options. From the east of the mountain there is a rarely used and indistinct route named after Njara, the small settlement from which it begins. It follows the Woma River to the Little Barranco on Mawenzi's eastern face but water and shelter are scarce at the higher altitudes and guides, on the eastern side of the mountain, might not be available. It is not a track for novices. A much easier alternative is to follow the regular Marangu Route, branching right after leaving Horombo Hut which takes you past Zebra Rock, and right again at a second fork where the track forks as it emerges on to the Saddle. Shortly afterwards the track splits again, the right hand fork bringing you to Mawenzi Hut at the western foot of Mawenzi itself, the left-hand fork heading north of Mawenzi Tarn Hut by the small stretch of water from which it takes its name.

Mawenzi Hut is a six person uniport, situated at 15,100 feet (4,600 metres) at the base of Mawenzi's West Corrie. Limited amounts of water are available from a stream flowing from the Corrie but there is no fuel and there are no lavatories. The huts at Mawenzi Tarn (there is a simply furnished structure of metal and wood and also a small uniport) are intended to house six people each. The huts, at 14,200 feet (4330 metres), are only half-an-hour's walk or so from Mawenzi Hut and almost due north of it, with water available from the tarn but no fuel or lavatories.

Mawenzi is often bypassed by walkers and climbers as they head for its more famous 'brother' across the Saddle, but there is much to be said for spending a little time in and around the two locations described above. The scenery alone is obviously different from that around Kibo and often just as rewarding. Iain Allen, for example, confirms that 'spectacular views down the Great and Little Barrancos can be obtained by climbing the scree behind the tarn' but he also warns that climbing on Mawenzi is hard from any side 'and there is no route to the top for an ordinary tourist as there is on Kibo'.

Most people choose to walk the White Mountain the 'easy' way, which isn't always easy. Whatever the route, every mountain is not only what it is, but what it is perceived to be. There are as many Kilimanjaro's as there are walkers and climbers and even to the same person, the mountain changes with perspective, time of year, and in different weather conditions. And mountains can be changed in other, less natural ways. Kilimanjaro, from every viewpoint and in the eyes of almost everyone who sees it, is a magnificent mountain. And yet those who admire it, and those appointed to guard its integrity have an awful responsibility. For what the Gods have created, Man can destroy.

Right: We made it!.

What the Gods have Created let no Man Destroy...

Environmental damage on Kilimanjaro and plans to reduce it

First the bad news...

Latest scientific evidence from the United Nations Intergovernmental Panel on Climate Change (March 2001) predicts that the icecap of Kilimanjaro will have gone within twenty years, because of global warming. One third of the ice has disappeared in the last 12 years and even if global warming, as some experts maintain, is part of a natural cycle, this is little consolation for those of us who know and love the mountain here and now. But Kilimanjaro itself, like its snows, is not eternal. Not even mountains last forever and what the Gods create, they can also destroy – Vulcan, of course, being a master of this ancient art. Man might not be capable of destroying a mountain as mighty as Kilimanjaro but he can destroy, remarkably quickly, much of its beauty and many of the life forms which make the White Mountain so fascinating and, to the Chagga and the Maasai and Tanzania in general, so valuable.

Mountains do not physically disappear, at least in the cosmic short term, but their ability to attract tourists – and dollars – certainly can. And the people who clamour to see or climb Kilimanjaro won't keep parting with their dollars if the mountain doesn't live up to their expectations. Hemingway's Kilimanjaro, 'As wide as all the world, great, high, and unbelievably white in the sun' might go on being wide and great and high, but its 'square top' might one day become unbelievably grey in the sun; the biggest colliery tip in the world. Not too many people would pay to spend five days on a colliery tip. Even the biggest tip in Africa. And yet, from top to bottom, Kilimanjaro has for many years suffered abuse and disfigurement, and has been taken for granted both by its Tanzanian caretakers and by the tourists themselves. There were times in the early 1990s, for example, when there were one hundred and forty people on the mountain, mostly on the Marangu Route, when there should have been sixty. Tourists complained of having to sleep on tables, or on the floor, in Mandara or Horombo. And were paying good money for the privilege. Some of the tourists themselves contributed directly to the problems. In September 1992 a party from the University of California walked the Marangu Route (used by about 91% of all visitors to Kilimanjaro) and found that :

'The rubbish was appalling! It was especially bad above 4,200 metres, where the desert started and no vegetation hid the mess. Plastic bags, water bottles, toilet paper, candy wrappings, sandwich paper and so on spread for over a hundred yards downwind of the track for hour after hour of walking. In Kilimanjaro's Forest Reserve, the threat came from elsewhere. A management plan, prepared in 1993 with the assistance of the Swedish International Development Authority and IUCN (The World Conservation Union), admitted that 'a laxity in management of the Kilimanjaro Forest Reserve has resulted in the over-exploitation of the montane forest'. It went on to list illegal hunting, honey gathering, tree felling, fuelwood collection, grass burning and incursions by domestic livestock as some of the problems at that time. The original rainforest has been greatly reduced over the years, with virtually the whole of the lower forest disappearing. The felling of hardwoods was banned by Presidential decree in 1984, after the excesses of the previous half century – much of which, of course, was prior to independence. The softwood plantations at Rongai and West Kilimanjaro alone resulted in more than 6% of the indigenous forest being cleared, and abuses continued, with local people sometimes indulging in unlawful logging operations and fuelwood gathering, causing noticeable thinning of the forest in certain areas. The area of impact was large. Deforestation leads, of course, to degradation of the water catchment among other negative 'spin off' effects. The lichens and liverworts and mosses which clad the trees and the ground with a water-absorbing cover are particularly important to the ecosystem, and yet with every tree that is felled and every clearance

Opposite: Porters and climbers in the Saddle.

Previous pages: Evening view of Kilimanjaro.

Cold Weather Care

Cold weather saps the battery strength of most cameras, so try to keep your camera warm at night by keeping it in your sleeping bag, or by carrying it under your parka or sweater as you climb up toward the summit. When entering warm huts from the cold outdoors, a plastic bag can be wrapped around the camera to prevent condensation from forming on it; the condensation will form on the bag instead. If the camera is cold – or frozen – rewind film slowly to prevent it from breaking.

Filters

At high altitude a Skylight filter (81A or CR1.5) will reduce the general bluish cast on the film. But if you are taking pictures of blue flowers, take the filter off to enhance the blue. In the forest, other types of skylight filters (81B and 81C) can reduce the bluish cast under the trees and enhance greens. Polarising filters are commonly used to enhance blue skies, but at high altitude often result in black skies on the final picture. Unless the exposure is properly compensated, polarising filters tend to darken the scene. Practice with polarisers before you go. Use them judiciously.

Exposure for Forests

Forests are beautiful to walk in, devilish to photograph. The reason is that the sun streaming through the leaves creates pockets of intense bright light in sharp contrast to the dark green shadows. The result is often that forest pictures look like a black and white chess board, with not much recognisable vegetation. To compensate for this, look for scenes that have roughly the same brightness and less contrast, such as a brightly lit leaf (but be careful of the bright reflections from leaves) against a patch of blue sky; or, a dark shadowy forest with no intense rays of sunlight beaming through. Or, make a decision: expose for brightness or expose for shadow, and let the other wash out or fade into darkness. Good forest pictures are rare.

Exposure for Snow

Snow is bright and it fools the built-in reflective light meters on most SLR cameras (if you are using a hand-held incident light meter you won't have this problem). You've probably seen that a lot of snow pictures are greyish; they are underexposed. The reason is that the light meter is set to assume 18% reflectivity from an object and adjusts the exposure accordingly. However, snow has 36% reflectivity, twice as much as the exposure meter thinks it has. Consequently, the exposure meter signals the camera to shut down the aperture of the lens 1 f-stop more than it should. It is counter-intuitive, but in a brightly lit snow scene, you compensate for the light meter and _open_ the aperture by one f-stop (for instance, from f16 to f11). You will have the correct exposure. Experiment before you go by taking pictures of a white piece of paper in the bright sun.

Start early, Finish late

The best light is early in the morning and late in the evening. The best landscape pictures are taken then and the rest of the day can be used photographing people, plants and small scenes that do not have much contrast or shadow in the bright midday sun.

All pictures by **David Pluth**;

(except pictures for **Mohamed Amin** on pages: 10, 23, 60, 62, 65, 66, 67, 69, 70, 88, 91, 99 *(below)*, 100 *(top and left)*, 103, 104, 105, 107, 109, 114, 117 *(left)*, 122, 125, 179;

and pictures for **Ian Vincent** on pages: 6, 12-13.